WHOLE EDUCATION

A New Direction to Fill the Relevance Gap

Raja T. Nasr

M.A., Ed.D., H.L.D., F.R.S.A.
Marymount University

UNIVERSITY
PRESS OF
AMERICA

Lanham • New York • London

Copyright © 1994 by

University Press of America,® Inc.
4501 Forbes Boulevard, Suite 200
Lanham, Maryland 20706

3 Henrietta Street
London WC2E 8LU England

Library of Congress Cataloging-in-Publication Data

Nasr, Raja Tewfik.
Whole education : a new direction to fill the relevance gap /
Raja T. Nasr.
p.   cm.
Includes bibliographical references and index.
1. Education, Secondary—Philosophy.   2. Education, Secondary—
Curricula.   I. Title.
LB1607.N216   1994   373'.01—dc20   94–21380 CIP

ISBN 0–8191–9609–6 (cloth : alk. paper)
ISBN 0–8191–9610–X (pbk. : alk. paper)

This book is affectionately dedicated

TO MY CHILDREN

Raif and *Randa*

Table of Contents

Foreword

I should like to begin by telling what happened to me as I read the manuscript of this book.

The first chapters deal with the problems confronting the educational community, the definition of "whole education", and the relevance of current education for the student. As I read it, I was convinced that the author, Raja T. Nasr, has a deep understanding of the educational process, and cares deeply about the schools and the students in them.

The teacher is described as a discoverer, a facilitator, a director and a counselor. I liked the descriptors. However, this is a big order for any person. It does indicate the importance of the teacher in the lives of the children and youth of our nation. The importance of planning and fitting the instructional style to the needs of the student population is described, and it is a sound one. I have been a teacher in the elementary school, the secondary school, university, both undergraduate and graduate school, and have developed many lessons and 15 years of experience teaching older adults, as well. There is no question in my mind that the teacher plays an important role in all four of the processes Dr. Nasr mentions. The teacher as a model of acceptable behavior in learning and in relationship to other people in this country and in the larger international context can influence students in positive ways.

The emphasis of **whole education** to each of the content areas such as language development, social studies, mathematics and science instruction is useful and can be of value in a variety of methods courses.

This book makes an important contribution to the integrated approach to learning content that is being emphasized across the nation. It also pulls together many ideas that will be useful to professional educators.

Martha Tyler John, Ed.D.
Vice-Chancellor
Africa Nazarene University
Nairobi, Kenya

Formerly
Dean, School of Education
and Human Services
Marymount University
Arlington, Virginia

Preface

It is commonly acknowledged that education is suffering - perhaps mostly at the secondary level - from a variety of ills. Some basic matters have gone amiss, making a growing number of students feel that the education they are receiving is not relevant and not touching their lives in a meaningful manner. This sad state of affairs is having serious consequences in our communities. Can something be done about it?

The answer is an emphatic and resounding *yes*, provided a concerted effort is made by all those concerned to rectify the situation. Educators should perhaps be the ones to take the initiative, but the solution will depend on the cooperation of the community as a whole. WHOLE EDUCATION prescribes a *new direction* on a number of fronts to restore meaningfulness and fill the relevance gap in secondary education.

It is hoped that some school or school system will adopt the basic principles suggested in WHOLE EDUCATION and provide a live example not only of how practical the steps are, but, more significantly, what differences (to the better) whole education will make in the lives of the students involved and in the general quality of life in their communities.

Chapter One

Introduction:
What Is It All About?

It is very evident that education today is suffering from a variety of ills. This is not to say that there aren't some very heartening and encouraging endeavors and activities in a number of schools in most states. Overall, however, there is a dire need for change. Perhaps there is one encompassing expression that can be used to typify the problem: education is suffering from a *relevance gap*.

Because education is suffering, our communities are hurting and the students are getting the short end of practically everything. Billions of dollars are being spent on education, and the problems persist: low academic standards, drop-outs, attrition, drugs, and crime. Motivation is lost. Politicians are scrambling for solutions and school systems are going around in circles unable to hit the nail on the head. Education seems to have lost its relevance.

Several ills loom large on the education scene. Practically every school district suffers — naturally in varying degrees — from lack of motivation on the part of students, lack of discipline, lack of respect for elders and peers alike, lack of interest in almost anything academic, attrition, absenteeism, drifting, low academic performance, lack of attention in class, tardiness, and dropping out of school. Standards in English are abominable; there has been negligible (almost nonexistent) improvement in reading skills between 1971 and 1990; for seventeen-year-olds, the reading skills have not reached the level of understanding, summarizing, and explaining "relatively complicated information," to say nothing about synthesizing "specialized reading materials;" writing proficiency is still at the minimal level. Standards in science and mathematics are pathetic; in mathematics, students are barely able to understand measurement and solve "more complex problems;" and in science, they are also barely able to understand and apply "scientific principles." In mathematics, U.S. students were heavily outscored by students in Korea, Taiwan, the Soviet Union, France, and Canada in 1991. (*The Condition of Education 1992*) The general standards in the social sciences and the arts leave much to be desired. The percentage of students graduating from high school is miserably low; the drop-out rate was about 7% between eighth and tenth grades and about 18% between tenth and twelfth grades in 1988-90; of the remaining students, less than 90% graduated from high school. (*The Condition of Education 1992*) The percentage of students enrolling in college work is even lower; those enrolling in college the same year they graduated from high school ranged from around 60% to 62.5% between 1988 and 1991 (*Digest of Education Statistics 1992*)

Some of the blame can, of course, be levied on certain domestic, social, and economic factors, but the bulk of the blame should rightfully be placed on educational factors. Education is simply not doing what it purports to do. The objectives are not met; the textbooks are too dry and rigid; the curricula are too stereotyped and straight jacketed; and, in many cases, the methodologies employed are too frigid. Education seems to have lost its relevance, and the students sense that something has gone amiss. No wonder apathy is so rampant. This relevance gap is more serious than one can imagine, and it needs to be addressed and redressed before it is too late. Where does the solution lie?

More money won't do it. (There is plenty of wastage as it is.) More books in the library won't do it. (The present holdings in many schools are not even dusted frequently enough.) More equipment won't do it. (Often the overwhelming supply of sophisticated equipment is not yielding proportionate benefits.) More staff won't do it. (There is a greater need for front-line personnel rather than behind-the scenes personnel.) More and better trained teachers won't necessarily do it if the view of the total program remains the same.

The national goals of education for the year 2000 are too general to give any real guidance to the direction that secondary education should take.   Of the six national education goals for the year 2000 (paraphrased),

Goal 1: *Readiness for school for all children*

Goal 2: *Ninety percent high school completion*

Goal 3: *Improved student achievement by grades four, eight, and twelve in all subjects*

Goal 4: *Highest scores in the world in science and mathematics for U.S. students*

Goal 5: *One hundred percent literacy for adult Americans*

Goal 6: *No drugs or violence in all schools,*

only two (namely, the "best" standard set for science and the general objectives set for the fourth, eighth, and twelfth grade levels) may be said to deal directly with the curriculum. (*America 2000*) Studies in 1990 and 1991 showing the likelihood of achieving these national goals by the year 2000 indicate dismally low prospects. (Elam, Rose, and Gallup, 1991) The other four (namely, readiness for learning, learning for life, the eradication of illiteracy, and absence of drug use) are essentially peripheral to a high school program and curriculum. Much more direct guidance is needed on the national level for high school education.

What is really wrong? We are approaching the twenty-first century, and our schools are still performing a very traditional role in an archaic methodology. When everyone — from politicians to community leaders, parents, teachers, universities, and the work place — is screaming about low academic standards, it is really a wonder why all this feedback is not making a dent in the educational system. We are still isolating the school from the life of the community; we are still compartmentalizing knowledge; we are still not giving proper individualized attention to students (with all that this implies), and we are still turning student assessment and evaluation into a mechanical routine that does not come close to ascertaining native talent and quality performance.

Because so much is organically wrong, students do not see much relevance or meaningfulness in what the schools are offering. Escape routes are sought continuously within the schools and in the community.

What is the solution? If we acknowledge the fact that something is basically wrong — especially with high school education — and if we are serious about rectifying the situation, then the first requirement is a mind-shift to a new mind-set. With a new mind-set, we would be prepared to look at secondary education not necessarily from scratch and with an absolutely new slate, but at least without any past prejudices and without any preconditioned attachments to old curricular content and disciplines and to traditional classroom methodologies. With this as a starting point, it would not require much wisdom and imagination to realize that two things are needed at the same time: a *directional change* and a *qualitative change* in the entire secondary school educational system.

Whole education prescribes both the directional and the qualitative changes needed to fill the relevance gap that speaks louder than words today and is the cause of many ills.

Chapter Two

What Is Whole Education?

There seems to be a tendency on the part of authors and also readers to want and expect a one- or two-sentence definition of a word or notion, especially if it is new or if it reflects something new. But such short definitions are hardly worth the words in them, because they fail to explain what is truly behind the definition. What is one to conclude, for example, from such definitions of education as "Education is life" or "Education is preparation for life" or "Education is a process of adjustment to problem situations" or "Education is a process of growth and development?" It is rather clear that definitions of this nature are grossly inadequate in spelling out what the defined term really means.

In an attempt to avoid such pitfalls and, more positively, to provide a better understanding of what is involved, a number of partial definitions of *whole education* are presented. Put together, these partial definitions help to spell out the various aspects of the nature and characteristics of *whole education.*

1. Whole education is preparation for abundant living. This is not meant to put anybody off. While the notion of having life "more abundantly" is Biblical in origin, there is a vital aspect of it that can be relevant and applicable to every person, student or non-student. To have life as such can be reduced essentially to sheer existence or a subsistence level of existence. This, of course, is relative. In some situations it could mean a bare subsistence type of existence with just enough food and drink not to perish. More progressively, it could include more sophisticated shelter, a job, schooling, some form of investment, material possessions, a decent social life, authority, position, a good reputation, and so on. "More abundantly" goes far beyond just "more" or "more abundance" of the above; it could mean inner satisfaction or contentment or self-fulfillment or moral stature or justification or faith or a promise of forgiveness and salvation or any combination of these.

Whole education does not impose any creed or faith or belief or dogma. It does, however, open doors for persons who can find meaningfulness in relating their faith to their whole selves and to their personal, social, vocational, and avocational lives. Every person has a spiritual aspect and nature. While this need may not necessarily be related to any organized form of religion, it should, nevertheless, not be neglected. Whole education addresses itself to the spiritual nature of students and provides wholesome channels for the development of this nature and for its effective integration with all other aspects of students' lives. Touching upon certain spiritual needs of students in the process of education is definitely not, in any shape or form, a matter of abrogating the principle of the separation of church and state.

2. Whole education is self-fulfilling. There has been much more talk than action related to self-realization. It is sad to witness lip service given to the idea of self-realization unmatched with enough or appropriate activity to ensure it. It is more disconcerting and, in some cases, quite appalling to see huge sums of money spent and innumerable programs set up with very little self-realization cash value in return.

Whole education starts out with the premise that the individual's potential is to be nurtured in order for it to blossom and be fruitful. Actualizing one's potential is a process requiring a variety of factors to reach fruition. These factors are

a. knowledge of oneself,
b. venues for growth and development, and
c. a conducive atmosphere.

Self-knowledge is the first step towards self-realization. Self-knowledge, as a result of consistent and sustained introspection, means knowledge about one's likes and dislikes, one's psyche, one's fears and anxieties, one's strengths and weaknesses, one's realistic ambitions, one's fanciful dreams, one's basic beliefs, one's moral code, one's concept of right and wrong, one's driving forces, one's complexes and inhibitions, and one's system of responses.

Probably one of the greatest challenges and responsibilities of teachers is to discover their students' real natures. It is on this basis that they can open up appropriate *venues for growth and development* for each of them. It is this knowledge on the part of the teachers that will make them realistically realize that the same lecture, the same assignment, the same activity administered to thirty students in class will be received, accepted or rejected, digested, integrated, implemented, and responded to in thirty different ways. Whole education makes it possible to vary the venues to suit individual learners.

Just as a plant needs much more than just the right kind of soil to grow and bear fruit, so students need much more than a school or activities to grow at an optimal rate and in an appropriate personal direction. A *conducive atmosphere* or *conducive climate* for optimal learning is essential. This atmosphere or climate is not only physical. The physical aspects of seating, temperature, lighting, equipment, software, and the like — important as they may be — are not as effective as the intangible aspects of the atmosphere. These include the attitude of the teacher, the personal and peer relations in class and in school, a sense of security in the total learning process, a sense of worth in class, a healthy and wholesome self-image coupled with a wholesome and balanced combination of firmness and friendliness in class. When such an atmosphere is provided, students can work effectively on their own levels and at their own speeds, feeling at ease in the process and enjoying a sense of accomplishment with their personal results.

3. Whole education is person centered. This is not a redundancy. It is not the same as saying that education is student centered. The emphasis is different. To say that whole education is *person centered* is to put the thrust and the emphasis on the individual person, the individual personality, the whole person. This personalism is to be seen as a dynamic whole within itself and a dynamic whole in its interaction with other persons and things and notions. Whole education does not only give lip service to this concept of personalism. In its activities and programs, whole education makes certain that the person — the whole person — understands herself/himself and sees herself/himself as a vital organism interacting effectively and meaningfully (and with impact) with the relevant concepts around, with other persons in the community (home, school, and society), and with all the elements of nature in the surrounding area. Whole education views each individual as a live personality influenced by and influencing ideas, nature, and other live personalities.

4. Whole education seeks balance and harmony. This again is not meant as a redundancy. To say that whole education seeks balance and harmony is to go way beyond the rather crude maxim that education is a process of adjustment to problem situations. If the focal point is the whole person, then a healthy and wholesome equilibrium must exist within every aspect of a person's life. The conflicts, the paradoxes, the tugs of war, and the imbalances abound. They exist on all levels and in all dimensions of life and existence. Human beings, as a matter of fact, are bundles of paradoxes.

Spiritually, intellectually, psychologically, and socially, humans carry paradoxes, imbalances, inconsistencies, and conflicts within themselves. They are at once gregarious and ego-centric; they are at once uplifted and filled with joy, pride, happiness, ambition, and love, and also desperately weighted down with sadness, deflation, hatred, anxieties, and fears; they are at once reasoning, though not always reasonable, beings; they are at once capable, through the grace of God, of being at one with Him, and also susceptible to devilish temptations pulling them constantly away from God. And they are forever confronted with choices — choices that, on the one hand, are partially determined by the struggles (within themselves) of these various paradoxes — and the choices that, on the other hand, determine, at every stage and to a very large extent, the direction of their future actions.

Additionally, there are numerous conflicts tugging away at persons, pulling them in all sorts of directions. Conservative and traditional views seem constantly to conflict with liberal and more permissive views; older patterns of behavior seem not to tolerate more trendy patterns; spiritual and materialistic values appear to be at war forever; selfish needs and altruistic drives sometimes pull people apart; absolute values and scales seem not to accept more pragmatic approaches; the "natural" way is often seen to be at war with the "synthetic," man-made, chemical, industrial, and commercial counterpart; and the struggle goes on.

All of these internal and external conflicts can tear people apart. Whole education endeavors to make students face these dilemmas head on, deal with them, come to terms with them, and develop an internal harmony and balance that can serve as a reconciler of external imbalances. Subjects are not taught as isolated spheres of knowledge, but as venues for handling real situations knowledgeably and effectively. But creating an internal and an external balance and equilibrium is not a one-shot deal; it involves a continuous effort. Whole education, as a process, equips students in imbalance and disharmony management.

5. Whole education is motivational. Because of the very wide scope of relationships and application implied in the methodology, whole education is in no need of external incentives to prod students to work. All the relevant incentives are imbedded in the content and methodology employed. Every student will find something to trigger her/his imagination and interest. Every student will discover something to make her/him tick. Every student will be able to identify with some aspect of the effort, the project, the endeavor, or the subject. And while each student may be reading, writing, or doing something different, all students in a particular class will be dealing with the same general theme, learning from others, and making a unique contribution to the group.

6. Whole education is integrative. The integrative scope of whole education is three-fold:

a. Whole education integrates different subjects. This integration goes way beyond the traditional view of cognate areas. Integration is not limited to such subjects as history and geography, language and literature, chemistry and biology, mathematics and physics, or art and music. Integration here cuts across all subjects. A war, for example, may be studied as the outcome of linguistic differences; a thorough study of a war would have to include considerable logistical information, requiring applied mathematical ability; a war can be seen to have human, humane, social, economic, geographic, political, educational, and scientific consequences; any material on a war can be looked at from a linguistic, literary, or artistic viewpoint; and any film on it can be viewed additionally from a dramatic angle. All subjects impact upon each other at different times and in varying degrees.

b. Whole education integrates subjects with life situations and circumstances. Mathematics, for example, can be made to be seen as a vital element affecting many aspects of our lives: budgets, pricing, buying and selling, temperature, speeds and speed limits, time and timing, weights, grades and averages, salaries and increments, investments and income, calories and dietary elements, medicinal dosages, radios, televisions, cars, machines, computers, industry, agriculture, astronomy, physics, space research and experience, and so on. Contrary to what is happening now in classes, every single student should find something very relevant in her/his life connected directly with skills in mathematics. Whole education focuses on this relevance in an integrative fashion to make all subjects come alive in different ways with different students.

c. Whole education integrates the objectives with the methodology in dealing with the content. The objectives of any course are never external to the course; they are to be seen as an integral part of the process or methodology used in teaching and learning the course. When we read a bit of news in a newspaper or magazine, we do not do it, obviously, to pass a comprehensive test on it. We immediately want not only to understand it, but, more importantly, to see how it impacts on our lives. The way we read the information, the interaction we have with it, and the consequent actions we take as a result are procedures that carry their objectives within themselves. So it is with whole education. The objectives, the content, and the methodology are so entwined with each other — so inseparable from each other — that they operate as parts and parcels of one whole.

7. Whole education is relevant. So much of what is included in various educational programs in different areas and on different levels has no relevance to students' lives. No wonder so many students feel disappointed, discouraged, and even despondent. In a huge number of cases, poor academic performance, attrition, and school leaving can be attributed mainly to the feeling that what is being said and done has little or no relevance to the live issues faced by students at home, in the community, and even in school. Whole education has its core in live issues and relates subjects and activities to these issues. Relevance is at the heart of the educational endeavor. Subjects and activities are conditioned by real issues and they have impact upon them at the same time. The relevance gap that exists in education today must be addressed and redressed immediately. Whole education purports to do just that.

8.   Whole education is meaningful. Because of the personal involvement of each student in relevant activities, whole education provides meaningfulness on three different, but closely related, levels.

a. Through the various activities they go through, students see their own lives as meaningful. And no person who sees her/his life as meaningful can give up, lose hope, or feel despondent.

b. Whole education makes students see their lives and activities as meaningful to others because of the interactions and inter-personal relations involved.

c. Life situations and conditions themselves — the good, the bad, the interesting, the disappointing ones — become meaningful because of the influence they have on individuals and because of the way they are influenced by individuals.

9. Whole education is introspective. The objectives, the content, and the methodology employed in whole education are oriented - partially at least - towards helping students gain an insight into themselves and discover themselves. This introspection is meant to make students understand themselves as a first step in the process of blossoming towards fulfillment. An introspective person is not necessarily an introvert, though even an introvert needs the insight of introspection to move ahead and make any desirable adjustments.

10. Whole education is "extroversive"/"extrospective". To say that whole education is introspective is only partially true. The corollary to this fact is equally true. Whole education is also extroversive/extrospective in the sense that it allows students - at their own speeds and in accordance with their own abilities, desires, and interests — to deal meaningfully with others and to turn the exchange and interaction into a mutually desirable and mutually beneficial undertaking.

What is whole education then? It is a movement; it is a new direction; it is a trend; it is an orientation; it is an attitude; it is an approach; it is a new educational mind-set; it is a way of thinking and behaving; it is a process that deals with knowledge, skills, attitudes, and emotions in a fashion that is not unrelated to the whole life and circumstances and conditions of individual students. It is a dynamic, live, interesting, self-fulfilling, balanced, harmonious, motivational, integrative, relevant, meaningful, introspective, and extroversive/extrospective way of handling the educative process, learning from the sum total of past experiences, living today fully and handling today's challenges adequately, and also looking forward to a brighter, more satisfying and more abundant life tomorrow.

Chapter Three

Whole Education and the Learner

1. Introduction

The focal point, the center of interest, the ultimate target of concern in education is — as it always should be — the individual student, the person, the personality, the learner. This has been acknowledged by educational philosophers, administrators, librarians, teachers, and staff members for a very long time now. An observation and examination of actual practice in schools and classrooms would indicate that there is little more than lip service given to this principle. If we are truly concerned about the total welfare and well-being of each individual student (spiritually, morally, socially, intellectually, and physically) as a learner, a worthy home member, a worthy member of society, and a responsible future leader and participant in civic duties and activities, much more needs to be done by the school system. To lose sight of those factors that make up the total well-being of the student, and to fail to relate all school-sponsored activities to those factors, serves only to enhance the irrelevance of any course of study and to widen the relevance gap already in existence.

Whole education is constantly cognizant of this fact and constantly striving to tie all the personal elements and characteristics of the individual learner to the various elements of the curriculum and also to the total life of the students as experienced at home, in the school, and in the community. Whole education would show real concern about a variety of related areas in the life of each student and attempt to do something concrete about them that would make the student know and sense her/his own relevance and the relevance of all the school-sponsored activities. All the points discussed below are to be viewed as constituting related parts of one whole.

2. Student Rights

Much is being said and written about student rights. Underlying and permeating quite a bit of what is expressed about student rights is a fear — often genuine and heartfelt — of what they represent actually and potentially. Some student rights —including the right to a free education once residence is established, the right of emotionally disturbed and otherwise disabled students to a free education as well, and the right not to be abused, molested, or harassed — have been regarded as very positive rights enhancing the well-being not only of students but also of various communities and the nation as a whole. Other rights — including the right to due process, the right not to be searched or have student lockers searched without cause, the right to free speech, the right to behave in any way akin to freedom of expression, the right not to be suspended without a hearing, the right to sue board members and seek damages from them, and the like — have only helped to inhibit and limit the scope of service rendered by teachers and administrators alike. In some cases, teachers and counselors have refrained from giving advice to students and parents lest the school be asked to pay for whatever is recommended.

All student rights are constitutional, and, if they are founded on the Constitution and Amendments, they should be upheld, honored, and practiced by all those concerned with the education of our youth. The question is not whether to accept or to fear student rights. The essential question is how to fully make use of these rights to enhance the well-being of students and their communities. The rights of students are not to be seen as standing in opposition to what the schools are trying to do; they are to be considered as an integral part of the total givens in an educational set-up. The rights are not a set of isolated laws; they are only parts of a whole situation, and parts should always be viewed in perspective and in relation to other parts. The students and parents who have taken undue advantage of some of these rights should be made to see the welfare of all students and their communities and to contribute as much as they can to it, instead of seeking unfair benefits. It is precisely as a result of practices of this nature that many loving and well meaning teachers have stopped patting students on the back, giving them a warm hug once in a while, or otherwise showing care and empathy. It is for the same reasons that teacher trainees have been warned against demonstrating genuine concern in any physical way lest it be taken as grounds for a court case. This is extremely unfortunate because the vast majority of students and teachers are missing a vital human and humane element in the educational process as a consequence of the behavior of a very small minority of students, parents, and sometimes deviant teachers.

3. Student Responsibilities

It is most dangerous to talk about student rights without immediately coupling rights with responsibilities. The give-and-take element involved in the combination is essential for everyone concerned. It is not as though students are at one end of the social spectrum ready and eager to receive and demand their rights from the other end and from the center of the spectrum. Students cover the entire social spectrum and structure; as such, they are recipients of their due, their share, and their rights; and, at the same time, they are doers, givers, producers, and contributors, sharing in the total responsibilities of their various sub-communities.

No sub-community — such as the home, the office, the church, the club, or the team — is without demands on its members. The demands take the form of understandings, consensus, rules, codes, by-laws, expectations, or the like; and they are there to ensure the smooth, effective, peaceful, harmonious, and successful operation of the activities. There is no demand on individuals that does not carry some limitation on freedom. But whoever is a part of a larger whole should expect various limitations of this type for the good of all, including the individual who is prone to fuss about such limitations. So should the case be in the classroom, in the laboratory, in the library, or on the playground.

These so-called limitations on freedom are not to be regarded by teachers, administrators, and students as "deprivations"; the expectations, the relationships between educators and students, and the general climate of a classroom or school should make all such "limitations" welcome, acceptable, and, in some cases, routine norms of behavior. In this respect, peer actions and mediation, especially with new students or with old students whose behavior is actually or potentially deviate, can have a very effective, resolving, preventive, or normalizing outcome.

4. Student Conduct and Behavior

The point here is not to discuss regimented behavior the way it is practiced in the armed forces or by the police; it is not even very uniform behavior as practiced by team players that is the focal point here. It is just normal, acceptable behavior as practiced in practically all aspects of our lives that is of interest now. In some offices, all men employees must wear coats and ties, and the coats must be buttoned when the employees move through the corridors; in some offices, all women employees must wear stockings and closed shoes; no (gum) chewing is allowed on the job by any employee in those offices. It is the law to buckle up in the front seat of a car; it is the law to drive on the right side of the road on two-way streets. Club members are, in most cases, required to produce their membership cards at the entrance. People queue up for almost everything where two or more people are involved. And so it goes. We are all immersed deeply in society and sub-communities that flood us with requests, requirements, demands, and regulations. Society, as we know it, cannot conceivably exist without such "limitations". Now to assume that student "rights" preclude them from having to conform to rules, expectations, or requirements is unrealistic. If education is truly full equipment for abundant living, the teachers and administrators who are generally permissive and lax in their demands and requirements are actually doing a gross disservice to their students; they are not preparing them for real life situations in the future, and they are, in a good number of cases, helping to produce rebels in society in the meantime.

There are very strict rules in the books about drugs and drug addiction. In too many cases, though, the rules are one thing and their actual enforcement is a far cry from the rule. But let us talk about much simpler matters. Why should there be any hesitation on the part of teachers to ask their students not to chew gum in class? Or to ask the boys not to wear caps in class? Why is there fear to demand as much respect from the students as the students think they have respect "rights"? Why should stealing a pen in a culturally diverse class not be addressed for fear of violating the respect due to cultural differences, when shoplifting by the same individual is considered to be more than a misdemeanor in society? The same, of course, is true of cheating and other vices. Why shouldn't all teachers and administrators require the use of proper and decent language, acceptable attire, and acceptable modes of general behavior? Is there, in addition, any reason why schools should not attempt to teach students the etiquette of good conversation, table manners, other social graces, and good human relations?

I was once asked by a school principal what I thought of his high school, which seemed to enjoy high academic standards and a wholesome social climate. I said, "Everything seems to be rosy here, but one thing puzzles me: Why are so many boys wearing caps in class?" He said, "I have discussed this matter with my teachers, and we wondered if we should crush the students' personalities by asking them to remove their caps." Crush their personalities? Nobody's personality is crushed when asked to obey a rule. On the contrary, the higher and nobler the expectation, the better the performance.

A definite and concerted effort is needed to spell out the minimum standards of acceptable social behavior, and an equally serious and concerted effort needs to be exerted to implement those standards in our schools. This "concerted" effort requires the cooperation of parents, students, teachers, administrators, and members of society at large.

5. The Student's Self-image

Nothing is more conducive to purposeful activity leading to concrete achievement than a person's good self-image. The opposite is also true: a low or demeaning self-image can very often lead to discouragement, apathy, despondency, and failure. A positive, healthy, and high but realistic self-image is a major key to success. Students who think they can perform, achieve, and succeed usually do so; and students who believe that the task is too difficult for them, that the stuff is above their heads, and that the goals and objectives are beyond their reach end up not exerting the required effort and meet with failure and disaster, to nobody's surprise - not even their own. Such students expect failure, and they are seldom disappointed!

The question is how to build a student's self-image. Naturally, there are some students who know themselves well enough, who have a pretty high regard for themselves, and who set rather high, though attainable, goals for themselves. These students expect success, and they achieve it. Other students, in varying degrees, lag behind in this respect, and they are the ones who need some attention both at home and in their schools.

To develop a student's self-image, a few principles should be observed. First of all, and most importantly, **be honest** with the student. Do not let her/him think that she/he can immediately attain the unattainable. Concentrate, instead, on what can be achieved, no matter how small or insignificant it is. This is not hard to do if you know the student's abilities and weaknesses. Secondly, **direct** the student's performance and activities toward achieving that goal, and **guide** her/him along the way by suggesting any necessary modifications in the process. Thirdly, **encourage** the student to persevere and follow through with the task until it is completed.   Fourthly, **praise** any measure of success that the student might meet with. And, finally, **look forward to and plan** another task that may be a shade more sophisticated than the preceding one.   Teachers who constantly and consistently **expect** their students to succeed and who match their expectations with the proper, individually-directed guidance are almost always satisfied with the results.

There is no student without potential and abilities. One of the biggest challenges facing teachers is to discover these abilities and this potential and to build on them in such a way as to make students come to grips with them, exert the required effort to fulfill them, and feel happy about who they are and what they can accomplish. Building a student's self-image honestly and objectively may be the strongest single factor contributing to success.

6. The Student's Worth to Others

Next in importance to a student's self-image is a student's worth to others: peers, teachers, relatives, and/or members of the community at large. A sense of being indispensable — no matter to what extent — can be a very big, sometimes the biggest, motivating factor to keep going, to keep up the effort, to seek, to strive, to accomplish, and to succeed. It therefore behooves the school and the teachers to see to it that every student has channels of activity to prove her/his worth to others.

Peer teaching, for example, is a real-life experience that has mutual benefits: the tutee learns, grows, and develops, and in so doing, provides the tutor with a value and a worth that she/he might otherwise not have. In this respect, the tutor's need for the tutee is just as crucial as the tutee's need for the tutor.

Special tasks assigned to specific students by the teacher to help with classroom chores or provide specific help in certain areas in class and in school can provide the students not only with bits of experience and responsibility, but also give them a sense of worth to others. Mowing the lawn for an elderly neighbor periodically is not limited in its value to the little money made on the side; the sense of worth it gives the student who does it is much more valuable than the material remuneration involved.

Examples abound of the channels available in school and in the community — albeit with some planning — to fill students' time meaningfully, to provide rich and practical experiences, and to demonstrate, first and foremost to the students themselves, their worth to others.

7. The Student's Goals and Objectives

It has been said that whoever aims at nothing, hits it every time. The apathy that is so prevalent in our schools and communities leaves many students with nowhere to go. Many seem to be aimless and hopeless. Whole education exposes students to a variety of venues and activities so actively as to make every student identify at least one interest to pursue in a meaningful way. When a student knows her/his own strengths as well as limitations and can channel her/his energies towards some end that will have meaning both to the student and to others, there will automatically emerge a goal or a set of goals in the mind of the student. In such cases, it is not necessary to start with an objective and then pursue some activities to attain it; by trying out a good number of venues and activities, the student might be able to develop a set of meaningful goals and objectives; and no student, or any other person for that matter, with a set of objectives — albeit attainable — can ever feel hopeless or despondent.

The idea is to have every student develop her/his own objectives, no matter how small or temporary, as a result of some introspection followed by self-projection through activities. Everybody gets involved, but not in the same way. Everybody gets involved in some activity with others. Whole education does not strive towards "busy-ness"; it strives towards involvement. And when every student is involved *in something with others*, personal goals and objectives are a natural outcome. Whole education provides each student with opportunities to develop her/his own personal and attainable objectives.

8. The Student's Channels and Activities

It is obvious that the channels open to students for meaningful activities lie in three separate, but related, areas: the school, the home, and the community at large. While this is obvious, it is not always made use of as fully as one would desire. An appreciable portion of a student's life is spent at home; but the home is, or should be, much more than a lodge. The home is, or could be, a dynamic place for wholesome interaction and growth as well as a source of comfort and security. The bulk of the student's waking hours during week days is spent in school. The rest of the time —namely, after school hours during the week and all through the weekends — is spent, at least partially, somewhere in the community.

There is a dire need to turn all three of these places (the home, the school, and the community) into much more dynamic areas of endeavor and interaction. They should come alive with activity; they should burst at the seams with interesting goings-on; and they should be much more receptive to the input of each individual student, who is at the same time a worthy home member and a member of society.

Whole education takes the initiative in school and, with cooperation from the home and various sectors of the community, attempts to channel student thoughts, activities, and endeavors in all three areas to develop a wholesome interaction between what is academic and the way or ways this academic base is used, employed, and implemented in the community at large.   (Specific suggestions and activities will be mentioned in later sections of this book.)

9. The Student's Interactions

In the physical world it may be true that to every action there is an equal and opposite reaction.   Applied to people, this would make relations very mechanistic. Growth and development come, in large measure, as a result of interactions. When there is interaction, there are at least two bodies dealing in some kind of exchange under certain given circumstances and conditions.

Two elements stand out as prerequisites for wholesome interaction: receptivity and productivity. Receptivity, at least on the surface, may give the impression that it is passive. For example, reading a passage may be termed a receptive activity based on one's general understanding of how the language functions and on at least a passive vocabulary. But this is not the real talent behind a reading activity.   The ultimate purpose in reading is to interact with the passage, and interaction requires a reaction of some sort — a kind of productivity. Do I agree or disagree with the passage? Do I like it or dislike it or parts thereof? Is it applicable to me? To what extent can I use it? What response do I have to it? Etc.

The same is true of any bit of knowledge or fact or activity that a student faces. If it is taken for its face value — if it is accepted just the way it is presented — if it requires no response of any kind — then it is a purely receptive and passive activity, and that can never in itself excite students or involve them in any way. If, on the other hand, students are given the chance to respond to, react to, or interact with that bit of knowledge or fact or activity in a way that brings them in contact with others, then there develops a dynamism and an involvement which can turn any fact or activity into something meaningful, applicable, and relevant.   That is a whole different cup of tea educationally. That is whole education.

10. The Student's Use of Time

How do high school students spend their time? It would be interesting to have a rigorous study on the subject. By roughly comparing students in the U.S. with students in some other countries (notably in Western Europe, the Middle East, and the Far East), it is not difficult to notice that the effort exerted by students in the U. S. on academic matters is dismally low. Homework and other after-school assignments are at a minimal level by comparison. When this state of affairs is coupled with the fact that students are, in general, not engaged in any other meaningful activity (such as hobbies, paid work, volunteer work, etc.) on a regular basis, no wonder there would be a tendency to resort to such escape routes as T.V. watching, loitering, taking to the streets or malls, or engaging in harmful, destructive, and/or unlawful acts.

If the school systems and teachers are depending (and putting more emphasis) on the native, innate talent of students, they must realize that for any native, innate talent or potential to come to fruition, there must be a *consistent effort* exerted on the part of the student, with the proper direction and guidance from the teachers, to *nurture* and *develop* such talent or potential. (See Staszewski, 1990) To begin with, more school time is needed for that. Students generally have a maximum of 180 (one hundred and eighty) school days, and the school day ranges from 4.5 to 5.5 hours. (*Digest of Education Statistics 1992*) In other countries of the world (Europe, the Middle East and the Far East, for example), the school runs to 3:00, 4:00, or 5:00 p.m., and the school days vary from 220 to 250. If international competition is being sought, school time should be substantially increased: daily to six hours and annually to at least 210 days.

The youth of high school age pack a staggeringly enormous amount of energy and vitality which needs to be tapped wisely and harnessed effectively towards positive and constructive ends. When this is not done, as is the case in too many situations, the energy can be directed towards negative, harmful, and destructive pursuits.

It behooves the schools and the parents (as well as the community at large) to see to it that a substantial portion of the students' after-school hours is spent

    a. on school-related and academically-oriented tasks and endeavors,

    b. on meaningful leisure-time activities such as sports, recreational

and social outlets, and the development of avocational interests, and
  c. on meaningful engagement and involvement in voluntary service
in the community.

Chapter Four

Whole Education and the Teacher

1. Introduction

In a sense, everybody is a teacher; we are all involved, at some time or another, in giving instruction, sharing knowledge, imparting advice or offering counsel. These are activities that practically all people indulge in whether in a classroom situation or in everyday life. While the following paragraphs may be directed primarily at school teachers and university professors, their essence applies equally well to everyone.

The choice of a one-word theme to symbolize the essential value of teaching is no mean task. Words like *superior* or *ideal* may be frowned upon by some. Even a word like *excellence* runs the risk of being redundant and over-used. So in an attempt to avoid frowns and risks and prejudices, I am using the word *excelling*, the *-ing* emphasizing action, growth, development, process, perseverance and continuity.

Excelling applies in three areas. The first area is academic excelling. A teacher's first responsibility, obviously, is to teach, and excelling in teaching lies primarily in superior instruction. Some of the implications of superior instruction are so obvious that they are often neglected. They include:

- a thorough knowledge of one's subject,
- a knowledge of sources and resources in the field,
- masterful and creative methods of imparting knowledge, skills, and attitudes,
- a just and impartial method of evaluating student progress and achievement in the subject, and
- a successful method of guiding and directing student study and growth in the subject.

But while superior teaching may be emphasized, let us not overlook (especially in the case of university professors) the significance of original contributions to the field of knowledge.   For university professors, then, academic excelling includes both superior instruction and worthy publications.

The second area is personal excelling. To say that a teacher's first responsibility is to teach does not mean that a teacher's sole responsibility is to teach. It is one thing to impart knowledge, skills and attitudes and another thing to develop creative, honest, responsible citizens and human beings with superior knowledge, masterful skills and wholesome attitudes.   A teacher's (and a professor's) role and responsibility go far beyond the textbook — far beyond the walls of the classroom — and far beyond the module, the semester or the year in which a course is offered.

Let your personal excelling as a teacher or professor take you beyond the mind, to the heart and soul of your students — beyond the school, to the community — beyond the textbook, to originality — and beyond the academic curricula, to life itself.

The third area is excelling in relationships. Because education is primarily a matter of human relations, there is no question in the minds of some educators that students, no matter what their ages are, can learn more from the personal encounter with their teachers and professors than from the words and information emanating from them. Important traits and characteristics of teachers and professors are, sooner or later, acquired by students. Part of you inevitably becomes part of them, just as part of them becomes part of you. What part of you would you like to see become part of them? What part of you would you like to see, if you had the choice, become universally part of everybody else? In other words, what part of you would you like to see "rub off"?

In discussing the disciplinary problem of cheating in an education class the week after the students had had an hour test with me on the "honor" system, one student asked, "Why is it that in certain classes students do not cheat?"

"The answer to this question," I replied, "hits at the core of what we have been trying to emphasize in education about attitudes towards knowledge, learners, learning, and teaching. The answer is simply this: that honest students will not cheat any way, and even potential cheaters would not normally betray a relationship of mutual trust and confidence once it is established between them and their tutors."

In a similar experience in a Teacher Training Institute, one student, exhilarated with her new and successful experience in self-reliance and self-confidence, remarked, "Sir, this is the way we are going to teach." "This is the way you must live," I said. "If you live this way, this is the way you will teach."

Some might think that this is being whimsical or dreamy or idealistic in a vacuum. It isn't. It may be idealistic, but in a very realistic and existential setting. I know; I've tried it, and it works. It works because this is life; this is everyday living; this is the stuff of being alive, of being in contact, of being concerned. And if, as Willmott says, "Education is the apprenticeship of life," then this is being teachers, tutors, professors, masters, counselors, advisors in the fullest sense.

And when this level of excelling is attained by teachers and professors then the whole world can be eternally indebted to them.

2. The Teacher's Vision of Her/His Role

Much of what was said above is the direct outcome of the teacher's self-image and vision of her/his role. If a teacher has a thorough grasp of who she/he is and some pride (not false pride) in what she/he stands for in terms of principles and goals, there is no doubt that a good measure of that will rub off on students and members of the community, giving added stature and respect to the teacher and added prestige to the school. This is not altruism or any form thereof. This is the business of running a teaching career successfully.

The teacher's success, to a very great extent, is measured in terms of student progress and achievement. In other words, each student's success is, to a high degree, the teacher's success. But what is student progress, achievement, and success measured against? Obviously, the objectives of the lessons, units, courses, and the curriculum as a whole must contain certain criteria to measure student success against. But if these criteria are made to mesh with the student's personalized goals, as whole education would prescribe, then there is a base for evaluation - a base for determining how well a student has performed. In the final analysis, and in very simple terms, the teacher's role is a combination of the following:

a.   to be a *discoverer* of each student's potential, interests, and goals;

b.   to be a *facilitator* of movement within the school and in the community, providing channels of action for the student;

c.   to be a *director* of activities and experiences, ensuring the student's growth and development in an appropriate direction for the student; and

d.   to be a *counselor* to the student, guiding the student's affective and behavioral conduct for optimal results. To have a genuine vision of this role marks half the way to success.

3. The Teacher's Planning

No plan works better than a plan for success. Teachers who plan for their own and their students' success are seldom, if ever, disappointed. But what are the major ingredients of a plan for success? Four major ingredients stand out:

a.   *Course, Unit, and Lesson Plans.*   These obviously, should include:
  • long-range common goals for the course,
  • a long-range plan of common student activities in the course,
  • medium-range common goals for the units in the course,
  • a medium-range plan of common student activities in each unit,
  • short-range common goals for the lessons in each unit, and
  • a short-range plan of common student activities in each lesson.

b.   *A Plan to Canvass the School.* This would be done for the purpose of:
  • locating source and resource material for student use,
  •   locating human resources that would be helpful in augmenting, applying, fortifying, reinforcing, and implementing theories, principles, and abstractions learned,
  •   discovering areas with potential openings for student activities and ventures, and
  • mapping out the various venues open to individual students or small groups of students to engage in.

c.   *A Plan to Canvass the Community.* This would be done for the purpose of
  • locating source and resource material for student use,
  • locating places of interest open to student visits (such as museums, galleries, zoos, industries, farms, offices, hospitals, clinics, nursing homes, shopping centers, police stations, fire stations, harbors, airports, bus and train terminals, civic centers, etc.),
  • locating human resources that would be willing to help in

supplementing, reinforcing, and implementing theories learned,
- discovering areas with potential openings for possible student activities and volunteer work, and
- mapping out such venues to tap when needed.

d.   *A Plan to Coordinate With Other Teachers.*   This would be done not only to ensure harmony in the total work of the school, but also to see that very little overlap, if any, is present and that no source or resource in the school or in the community is overtaxed.

When a teacher's planning covers all these four areas, four major advantages emerge: the curriculum in the whole school gains much more cohesiveness, the school becomes a much greater integral part of the community, the teachers feel they have a higher and broader scope to work in, and the students develop a sense of excitement and relevance in what they are doing.

4. The Teacher's Relationship With Students

The biggest single factor affecting student learning and behavior in the educative process is, doubtless, the relationship that the teacher holds with students. Much has been said and written about this, but the whole education approach makes it imperative to foster a wholesome relationship that would be conducive to optimal learning, growth, and development.   A wholesome relationship is established when the following principles are adhered to as closely as possible:

a. The teacher's own behavior is a model. Ultimately, it is not what is preached that counts; it is what is practiced.

b. While all teachers, as human beings, have their likes and dislikes, students should be treated fairly and equitably without any obvious favoritism, bias, or prejudice.

c. There is a balancing act to be maintained. It is important for teachers to balance firmness and friendliness in their total behavior with students. The consequences, otherwise, will not always be happy ones.

d. An attitude of professionalism coupled with professional behavior with students, peers, and members of the community goes a long way towards maintaining standards.

5. The Teacher's Teaching Style

Every teacher has a particular and personal teaching style. Some lean more heavily on one or two style forms, while others use combination forms in their teaching. The various factors influencing one's teaching style are: lecturing, presenting, explaining, question-asking, discussing, quizzing, testing, working with individuals, working with groups, emphasizing facts and knowledge, emphasizing understanding and implementation and application, relying on class work, relying on homework and out-of-class assignments, being a strict disciplinarian, having more relaxed discipline in class, being very permissive, using learning aids, insisting on active student participation, pacing in the classroom or taking a stationary position, being emotional or objective, being serious or jovial, etc. Learning is somewhat enhanced when the student's learning style does not conflict with the teacher's teaching style. The teacher, of course, is more in control of this matter than are the students.

Whole education does not necessarily prescribe any one teaching style, because teachers, as is the case with the students' learning styles, need to develop their own teaching styles as effectively as they can. A few suggestions, however, may be found helpful in making whole education more effective and successful.

a. Try to vary your teaching style as much as possible not only to lessen the repetitiveness and boredom of using one style consistently, but also to try and give every student the opportunity to respond rather positively with her/his own learning style.

b. Try constantly to relate what you are doing and how you are doing it to the integrative purposes of whole education.

c. Inject into your teaching style the affective element of caring, because students will have the tendency to respond to this element more personally and meaningfully than to any other aspect of your teaching style.

6. The Teacher's Evaluation of Student Progress

One of a teacher's most important responsibilities is to grade (mark) and evaluate student progress and achievement. While this section is not meant to prescribe a new trend in evaluation and measurement, it is, nevertheless, important to point out four basic principles involved in the process of evaluation and measurement only in the interest of having the whole education approach yield the best results and outcomes possible.

a. *The Importance of the Objectives*
No evaluation can be meaningful unless it is matched against the stated

objectives. It is of utmost importance to keep in mind three elements contributing to and affecting any stated objectives in the whole education approach: the integration of subject areas, the integration of the curriculum as a whole with real life situations and experiences, and the personal interaction that each student has with the curriculum and different aspects of community life.

b. *Maintaining Standards*

It should be very clear to teachers and students alike that obtaining results (behavioral and affective) is the object of the educational operation. Just as clearly stated should be the assigned or arbitrary grade value: C, D+, 75, 70, etc. Performance above or below this standard can then be more easily assessed. Standards should be set from the start, and it should be remembered that tampering with marks (up or down) after the fact (i.e., after students have performed) does not at all change the facts about the actual performance; it only betrays the original standard set. If a test or assignment is found to be too easy or too difficult, it is better to scrap it entirely or repeat it or modify it rather than to play with the marks and distort the real meaning of the actual performance.

c. *The Importance of the Individual Student*

Within the framework of the objectives and the standards to be maintained, it is important to see to it that each student is also evaluated individually rather than in competition with others. This is more a matter of attitude on the part of the teacher than it is a mechanical process, but it is an attitude that rubs off on students and that can influence their academic and personal performance. From actual teaching experience, there is testimony that student performance improved — in some cases, very measurably — when they stopped wanting to be *the* best and concentrated on being *their* best. From this point of view, ranking students in class can very often be more than meaningless; it can be harmful, with serious adverse effects. "Within the framework" at the beginning of this paragraph is meant to show that all these three matters are to be observed together and balanced in a practical, meaningful, and effective manner.

d. *Evaluative Assessment*

Schools and school systems practically around the world have been oriented to student assessment in quantifiable terms. Passing criteria, promotions, transfers, graduation requirements, scholarships, and the like are determined by some average or mathematical formula. While this is likely to continue, let us not forget the great significance of a personalized evaluative assessment of a student's work, abilities, and achievements. Statements pertaining to *attitude, cooperation, personal and social behavior, weaknesses, strengths, special abilities and talents, special accomplishments,* and the like would go a long way to telling who the person really is and what she/he can achieve and accomplish. When such statements are accompanied with words of *commendation* (regarding strong points) and *recommendation* (regarding points to be improved), then we have what might be termed a truly *authentic evaluative assessment* of the student. This, after all, is what interviewers and employers are really interested in.

Some school systems are experimenting with innovative ways of testing and evaluating student progress and performance. It is definitely not satisfactory to make passing critical objectives the ultimate goal. Much more needs to be done in this respect experimentally first and then on a nation-wide basis. More effective ways should be devised to assess student abilities and performance, as objective and standardized tests fall short of giving all the information desired.

7. The Teacher's A, B, Cs

For whole education to produce optimal results, the teacher's A, B, Cs should be observed. They are:

• *A for Ability.* A teacher's competence, while it is not the only qualification of importance, is probably the first element to be assessed. While the *A* stands primarily for *ability,* it can and should also stand for *accessibility, adjustability,* and *agility.*

• *B for Broad-mindedness.* Nothing is more limiting to the teacher or more frustrating for the students than a narrow-minded teacher. A teacher must have wide horizons and be very accommodating. While the *B* stands primarily for *broad-mindedness,* it can and should also stand for *belief* (at least in the dignity of all human beings), *belongingness* (at least to a home, a system of education, and a community), and *benevolence*(at least in heart and mind).

• *C for Caring.* One of the first elements that students respond to positively is the teacher's sense of caring in general, but at least for the students and their welfare. While *C* stands primarily for *caring,* it can and should also stand for *challenge, civility,* and *confidence.*

- *D for Dedication.* Teachers who are not committed to their profession wholeheartedly cannot be expected to perform optimally. While the *D* stands primarily for *dedication*, it can and should also stand for *dependability, diligence,* and *discipline.*
- *E for Effectiveness.* Effectiveness is output-oriented, result-oriented, outcome-oriented. While the *E* stands primarily for *effectiveness*, it can and should also stand for *efficiency, eloquence,* and *empathy.*
- *F for Firmness and Friendliness.* The proper balance between friendliness and firmness can spell success for the teacher. While the *F* stands primarily for *firmness* and *friendliness*, it can and should also stand for *facilitation, fairness,* and *fluency.*
- *G for Growth.* This is growth on the job and growth professionally. While the *G* stands primarily for *growth*, it can and should also stand for *gentleness, glamour,* and *guidance.*
- *H for Honesty.* Honesty is not only the best policy; it is an absolute must for teachers. While the *H* stands primarily for *honesty*, it can and should also stand for *helpfulness, hopefulness,* and *humaneness.*
- *I for Integrity.* This applies to personal, social, and professional integrity. While the *I* stands primarily for *integrity*, it can and should also stand for *imagination, improvisation,* and *industriousness.*
- *J for* (Good) *Judgment.* It is most important for teachers to demonstrate their wisdom by making wise choices and judgments. While the *J* stands for good *judgment*, it can and should also stand for *jauntiness, joyfulness,* and *justice.*

8. The Teacher's Professional Growth

There is no such thing as a plateau for teachers professionally. One either improves and grows or backslides. Backsliding should not be permitted. The only way for teachers to go is up, both personally and professionally. This point, however, is not to be limited to the traditionally accepted and followed venues for growth: added credits, certification, higher degrees, exchange programs, workshops, seminars, and the like. In *addition* to these, teachers using the whole education approach should try other methods of growing on the job, particularly because whole education has no set formula or prescription methodologically. It would be helpful to teachers to pursue one or more of the following at all times: read more on the subject; exchange views with other teachers using whole education; use exchange class visits; be open to suggestions from students and parents; discuss the whole education approach with members of the community for information and input from them; experiment with new methodologies and techniques; and try to vary classroom procedure by using your imagination and innovative resourcefulness as much as possible. (See Blaisdell. 1993)

9. The Teacher's Time and Schedule

Teachers are at a great disadvantage, given their teaching schedules and list of assignments and responsibilities. The system strikes the teachers with a double-edged sword: to keep up with their tasks and responsibilities (meeting with their department colleagues, meeting with other colleagues in faculty gatherings, planning their lessons and units, preparing the necessary learning aids, meeting and teaching their classes, dealing with too many students in various classes per day, staying on to counsel students, assuming other school duties such as monitoring the halls and watching over students at lunch time, contacting parents and meeting with them when necessary, evaluating student performance, and submitting the required reports), no wonder teachers feel physically and mentally exhausted; and, because their material remuneration is desperately below the desired level (even merit pay is discontinued when school budgets are tightened), they feel morally drained. Sometimes, to make up for low and/or insufficient pay, teachers seek outside part-time employment, which, of course, further saps their energies and demoralizes them as teachers.

In some other countries, especially ones with higher student performance and achievement, teachers spend much more time planning their courses and much less time in actual teaching. As a result, and as part of their planning strategies, they spend much more time meeting and cooperating with colleagues to coordinate and integrate their work. The students, of course, are the recipients of a better quality education this way, and the teachers are less tired and have a greater sense of achievement.

The structure of the current system in high schools needs to be changed radically. Tackling the situation from one end only will not do it. The problem needs to be faced on all fronts. The elements in the system that need modifying and, in some cases, overhauling, are the following (taken together):
• The teaching load needs to be adjusted (downward) to allow for more preparation time (including integration work with colleagues).
• The nature of the teaching assignments (in terms of course content)

needs to be reworked and overhauled to allow much greater emphasis on a core curriculum with a meaningful integration of different subjects in the curriculum and a practical integration of academic work with real-life experiences.

• Enough time will need to be allowed (at least for some teachers in the school system) to arrange coordination and integration between academic work and community experiences.

• Instead of having the traditional administrative setup of department chairpersons, it may be much more productive to have area coordinators (in charge of major integrative concerns) and coordinating assistants (in charge of working out student schedules and assignments in school and in the community).

Whole education is performance oriented; it is production oriented; it is result oriented. With the changes suggested above, it will be possible to have a system with a thrust on action, performance, practical results, higher academic standards, and more meaningful and more relevant experiences. The teachers will feel more enthused about their work: it will be much more relevant and interesting, and the results will show a dramatic move upwards.

Chapter Five

Whole Education and the Curriculum

1. What is the Curriculum?

Many people mistake a course of study for the curriculum; and, conversely, many think of the curriculum in terms of courses of study. A course of study is, naturally, a part of the curriculum, but the curriculum is more than just the sum total of all the courses of study. Any activity undertaken by a school as a part of its program with the intention of having it serve as a vehicle towards achieving its goals is, for that matter, a part of the curriculum. In this respect, no activity sponsored by a school is extra-curricular. Any activity sponsored by a school — whether it is conducted in class, in the laboratory, in the library, on the school grounds, or in the community — is curricular. The curriculum, then, is made up of all the programs and activities directed under the aegis of a school as part of a process to achieve its educational objectives.

2. Integrating the Curriculum

Integrating the curriculum is a must. Without proper integration, the curriculum of any school can become a fragmented mosaic of bits and pieces of courses and activities loosely bound together by a school schedule. The integration of the curriculum should be done with the students (primarily) and the teachers (secondarily) in mind as constituting a community working together and sufficiently motivated to achieve desirable results. (See Short and Burke, 1991)

The traditional concepts and practices of vertical and horizontal integration are fundamental, but minimal. To integrate the curriculum vertically is to ensure that, in terms of objectives and content at least, each subject area is properly graded and sequenced throughout the school system. The objectives should be stacked logically and sequentially upward through the grades. Similarly, the course content at each grade level should be designed in such a way as to have a smooth flow of it through the grades — perhaps allowing for some overlap or review possibilities at the beginning and at the end of each course. To integrate the curriculum horizontally is to ensure that at each grade level the various subjects and loads are streamlined in such a manner that the students see a relationship among the subjects and that all subjects require a commensurate level of logic, language proficiency, and other necessary skills.

In many cases, only lip service is given to vertical and horizontal integration. But even where something is being done, it is usually limited to the bare minimum requirement of having a certain number of departmental meetings (where vertical integration can be touched upon) and grade teachers' meetings (where horizontal integration can be touched upon) during the school year. Obviously, even in these two traditional areas of integration, much more can and should be done. Here are just a few examples:

a. *Note Taking.* What a marvelous opportunity teachers have to train secondary school students in note-taking. It takes just a bit of a coordinated effort among teachers and just a few minutes periodically in different subjects (especially English, history, geography, and the sciences) to prepare students to be first-class note-takers in college. In the meantime, of course, the training is extremely helpful in making students concentrate on the subject and sift out the essential points from the peripheral and secondary bits of information. All it takes on the part of the teacher is an occasional question like, "From the presentation I have given in the last ten minutes on ..., what have you taken down as important points?" Periodically, of course, it would be good for the English or social science teacher (by agreement) to check each person's notes for some advice and feedback.

b. *Report Writing.* In all subjects where student reports are expected and assigned, it would be beneficial to require the same format and style (MLA or APA). Apart from making the writing requirements less confusing for students, picking one style and adhering to it helps develop the students' sense of academic discipline, their scientific approach, and their artistic and/or literary styles; it also reduces the possibilities of plagiarism.

c. *Library Use.* The library is said to be the heart of any school, college, or university. It is truly regretful to witness the fact that in too many schools the library is, in effect, nothing but a necessary and required appendix. It is regretful not just because of the high cost of maintaining a library with its books, periodicals, films, media, and staff, but more so because of the very small number of students who frequent the library or make use of its enormous potential as a media center and learning resource. With a concerted effort on the part of the teachers, students in high school should use the library between three and ten hours a week to study, read newspapers and periodicals, make use of the references (dictionaries, encyclopedias, maps, etc.), begin to do in-depth research, do some interdisciplinary studies, check books out, and tap the library staff as resource personnel. With a wide variety of topics, projects, studies, and ventures to choose from in a variety of courses, students (individually or in groups) should, on their own, but with guidance from their teachers and the library staff, turn the library into a dynamic center of learning, continuously buzzing with meaningful activity. The interdisciplinary studies and projects can be guided by two or more teachers at the same grade level.

   d.   *Homework and Assignments.*   Students in some classes are overburdened and often overwhelmed by the different homework assignments given to them by certain teachers. In some cases, it is one or two teachers who exercise a monopoly over homework. The coordination and integration of these assignments would result in more balanced work at home in terms of quantity and content spread. To a certain extent, agreement among teachers about deadlines and formats would be helpful to students in many ways.

   Examples such as the above constitute the bare minimum of vertical and horizontal integration. But whole education requires much more in the way of curricular integration. A very big factor contributing to the irrelevance of the curriculum to students' lives is the tendency on the part of the students and teachers to compartmentalize and departmentalize the subject areas, as if they are entirely unrelated to each other. Much more relevance can be injected into the curriculum by considering integrative matters and factors such as the following examples, expressed in question form. (These and others are developed in greater detail subsequently.)

   • Why can't the English class allow the development of readings, themes, and essays related to the history or geography content in the social science class?

   • Why can't the language, science, and mathematics teachers

cooperate on assignments to be presented orally and/or in writing dealing with famous mathematicians and scientists in history?

• Why can't a history class studying a particular situation in some country or state at a given time handle assignments dealing with the scientific knowledge available at that time and how that might have affected life in general, communication, transportation, and logistical matters related to battles and wars?

• Why can't the arts and crafts class prepare materials that would be helpful in other courses (flash cards, learning aids, attractive bulletin boards, maps, tables, handouts, etc.)?

• Why can't a mathematics class do actual budgetary and other calculations related to student enrollment, the football team, social activities, school buses, the library, and the like?

• Why can't a drama production develop interdisciplinary experience by having students handle script writing, rhetoric, a social problem, costume design, stage setting, lighting, the budget, and human relations?

3. The Component Parts of Education

In economics we talk about the three factors of production: land, labor, and capital. Naturally, production could come to a standstill or, at best, be very crude and meager, if these three factors of production were not brought together in some production design under management or organization. Similarly, in education, there are three component parts ("factors of production", if you please) that go hand in hand towards "producing" the desired educational services in a community. These component parts are the aims and objectives of education, the curriculum, and the methodology employed. The first of these factors (aims and objectives) represents the *why* of education; the second (curriculum) represents the *what* of education; and the third (methodology) represents the *how* of education. Here again these three component parts are brought together through educational administration. In essence, then, it is the administration that puts together the *why*, the *what*, and the *how* of education along with the *who*, the *where*, and the *when*.

The aims and objectives (the ultimate, the proximate, and the immediate) of education come first. They serve to give a sense of direction and a sense of purpose. Whether educators and philosophers champion fixed or more fluid aims, the fact remains that it is the aims that would affect and ultimately yield a set of activities (the curriculum) that would serve as a vehicle towards achieving the aims and objectives.

Both the aims and the curriculum would influence the methodology used to arrive at the goals. This has been accepted for a very long time. The tragedy, however, lies in the fact that many of the basic aims and objectives, once stated, are lost sight of in the process. As a result, the *component* parts become fragmented, adding much to the relevance gap in education today.

4. Integrating the Component Parts of Education

In whole education there is a conscious and continuous effort to integrate the three component parts of education. For example, in a physics class, if one of a lesson objectives is to understand the law of falling bodies, would it not be much more effective, interesting, and relevant to do the following: explain the fascinating story of how, for a few hundred years, the people in Europe learned that objects twice as heavy as other objects would fall twice as fast (very logical on the surface); tell how Galileo Galilei thought there must be something rather faulty with that logic and how he experimented with two objects, dropping them from the Tower of Pisa with no measuring instruments; explain the present physical law of falling bodies; have students observe and do experiments in the laboratory, using precise instruments; and discuss the different ways in which this law of falling bodies affects us practically in our daily lives? This way, the law of falling bodies ceases to be just a formula to be memorized in a physics class; it becomes a meaningful experience, relevant to everyday life, and a part of the students' understanding and behavior. For another example, take a unit on the French Revolution in a world history class. Here are a few suggestions in terms of activities and methods that will make the objective of understanding the French Revolution an integral part of the students' lives and behavior: based upon a variety of readings, let the students discuss the causes of the French Revolution, let the students, in class presentations, depict everyday life in France prior to and during the Revolution; let some students make a map of France to be used in class; let other students (who may be artistically inclined) draw scenes depicting life among the royalty, life among the farmers, and the guillotine; discuss the outcomes of the French Revolution in France and its influence on other parts of Europe; discuss some similarities or differences in other later revolutions or civil wars; and discuss the various possible forms the French Revolution would take if it were to take place today. When history is taught and learned this way, students will, in time, see history as a part of themselves and themselves as products of history; they will also be able to understand and appreciate present events around the world and, to a certain extent, predict future trends. This is a completely different ball game from viewing history as a series of (often unrelated) dates and events. For a third and final example, take the reading of a novel such as *The Scarlet Letter* in an English class. After reading the novel at home, let the students discuss the different characters; let them see how literature mirrors the thoughts and feelings of a people in a given place at a given time; let them try to discover how similar characters would fare in their own communities today; let them write about some aspects they liked and/or disliked; let them discuss the author's style and compare it with the styles of other authors they have read; and let them act out (in their own words) certain scenes and incidents from the novel. Going through these activities in such a method would bring to life and fruition some objectives like improving their understanding of an age, widening their vocabulary, improving their styles, interacting with a piece of literature and expressing opinions freely and responsibly. The objectives of creativity and language proficiency would be realized in an interesting, dynamic, real-life fashion.

One can go even further. In many cases, as a matter of fact, it is not only a matter of putting together three different component parts of education; it is, rather, a matter of seeing any two or all three of these component parts as one. For example, a good number of courses would include, among their objectives, one or more of the following: objectivity, free expression, intellectual honesty, creativity, cooperation, free choice, responsibility, civic responsibility, human relations, etc. If the methodology employed by the teacher is in itself very much in line with these objectives (i.e., if the teacher is objective, intellectually honest, creative, cooperative, responsible, a good model of behavior with good relations with superiors, peers, and students; and if the teacher allows students to express themselves freely and gives them opportunities to be creative and cooperative and responsible), then the objectives can be enhanced and the students will grow in their development and mastery of these objectives. Otherwise, the methodology itself can be the biggest factor undermining those very objectives. It would be just like having a liberal education course taught by a narrow-minded, bigoted, prejudiced, straight-jacketed individual. It will not work as well as when the objectives and the methodology (and, to a certain extent, the content) are in harmony with, and inseparable from, each other.

5. The Major Problems of the Present Curriculum

It is very evident that substantive changes need to be made to the present secondary school curriculum. The major areas in which change and reform are most needed are the following:

• The length of the school day (generally under 5..5. hours.) needs to be extended at least one more hour.

• The length of the school year (under 180 days) is dismally low compared with school years in other countries. This needs to be upped to at least 210 days.

• In all education courses, it is taught that the aims and objectives determine the content (curriculum) to be prescribed and the methods to be used. In practice, however, this is not the case. The objectives are there on paper. The textbooks, which are extremely limited in number for any desirable choice to be made, dictate the content; they actually *become* the curriculum. This is particularly true of mathematics, the sciences, and the social sciences. The aims ultimately boil down to finishing what is in the textbook. As a drastic consequence methodologically, the teachers resort to emphasizing the *emission* and *transmission* of information and knowledge, rather than delve into processes of *transaction* and *interaction*.

• To set national standards (as minimal goals) in all areas of academic endeavor and to devise methods of assessing student achievement (against these standards) are of the greatest importance. (National Council on Education Standards and Testing, 1992)

• The aims and objectives should be clearly spelled out, and they should be given much more than lip service. The curriculum should then be set; and after that, textbooks should be prepared to achieve the aims and fit the curriculum. Many more textbook choices should be available to teachers and administrators to choose from. (See Marsh, 1992)

• The curriculum itself should exhibit more differentiation. Just as we have differentiated teaching and differentiated learning, so there should also be a differentiated curriculum meeting the different needs, interests, and learning styles of students. (See Page and Valli, 1990)

6. Whole Education and the Curriculum

Whole education plans for success; it plans for the success of the educational operation, but, of course, not for its own sake; the success of the educational operation is focused on the success of each individual student. In terms of the curriculum, then, whole education plans consciously and continuously to integrate the elements involved on three closely related levels:

a. It plans to integrate the curriculum vertically and horizontally in a much more profound manner than has been traditionally the case — especially and additionally in interdisciplinary areas.

b. It plans to integrate the three component parts of education in a very down-to-earth and effective manner, bringing in the administration as an active participant in the process.

c. It plans to integrate all the elements of the curriculum and the component parts of education with the actual life of students in the community. (This last point is discussed more fully in a subsequent section.)

Chapter Six

Whole Education and the Language Arts

1. Introduction

On the surface, the above title might give the impression that all we are interested in is whole language. While there is definitely a great interest in, and much to say about, whole language, an attempt is going to be made to show that whole language is just the bare minimum expected in a whole education approach. To deal with the subject systematically and in a way that will make it easier to understand, a presentation of six sub-topics will be made: (a) the component parts of language, (b) the language skills, (c) the use of language, (d) the major objectives of teaching and learning the language arts, (e) the determination of the methodology to be employed, and (f) whole education and the language arts.

2. The Component Parts of Language

Reference is usually made to two elements related to language use: form and content. Form means the shape, the structure, the style of the language act, and content refers to its meaning. There are some who would consider meaning (content) as one of the component parts of language. Naturally, all language use is intended to elicit some meaning. Any discussion of language without reference to meaning is pointless from an applied linguistics angle. In this section, however, the component parts of language are restricted to form. Meaning (content) will be handled later. The presentation will be brief and to the point.

The component parts of language form are three: phonology, morphology, and syntax. There is a great advantage, as we shall see shortly, in using the word *morphology* instead of the word *vocabulary*.

The *phonology* of a language is its sound system. The word *system* is used because phonology is just that: a sub-system of sub-sub-systems in a language. The element (sub-system) of English phonology has two main branches (sub-sub-systems): the segmental features (consonants and vowels) and the supra-segmental features (stress, intonation, pause, juncture, and rhythm). These work together in patterns and in specific sequences to make up the sound system of English. For example, let us take three consonants (/t/,/s/, and /r/) and two vowels (/i:/ as in m*ea*n and /i/ as in f*i*n). Now by using different combinations of these sounds to form English words, we come out with *sit, seat, its, eat, eats, east, steer, tear* (of the eye), *treat, treats, street, streets,* etc. But no English word can be formed if it starts with *ts* or *rs* or *sr* or *rt* or if it ends with *sr* or *str* or *tr*. Other languages having the same three consonants and two vowels may allow initial or final clusters that are not found in English. Now all the consonant and vowel sounds (phonemes) are in contrast with each other. The following words are all different because the initial consonants (phonemes) are contrastive: *pin, tin, thin, sin, fin, bin, shin, kin, win, chin, gin, Lynne,* etc. These examples illustrate that contrastiveness and structured sequencing are of paramount importance in phonology.

The branch of supra-segmental features consists of the following:

• *Stress* (force of breath) which applies to words and to larger utterances. Notice, for instance, the difference in the stresses in the following pairs of words: *perfect* (adjective)/*perfect* (verb); *subordinate* (adjective)/*subordinate* (verb); *compose*/*composition*. Also notice the shift in the sentence stress when the following sentences are read in pairs:

> *My brother didn't eat the apple./Your brother did.*
> *My brother didn't eat the apple./My sister did.*
> *My brother didn't eat the apple./He sold it.*
> *My brother didn't eat the apple./He ate the pear.*

• *Intonation* (pitch of the voice) which adds meanings to utterances. For example: (finality) *He arrived yesterday.* (question) *He arrived yesterday?* (surprise) *He arrived yesterday!*

• *Pause* (tentative or final) which applies in utterances. For example: *When he arrived* (tentative), *we left* (final).

• *Juncture* (minuscule stoppage between words or parts of words). Notice the difference between the following pairs: *nitrate/night rate, I scream/ice-cream.*

• *Rhythm* (a combination of the above to show the beat in utterances). Every language has its own rhythm.

The second component part of language form is *morphology*, which is a study of word forms and their changes. A morpheme in a language is its smallest meaningful unit. For example, the word *cat* and the word *cats* are both words. But the first one (*cat*) is composed of one free morpheme, and the second is composed of two morphemes: a free morpheme (*cat*) and a bound morpheme (s). All the prefixes and suffixes are generally bound morphemes. In English, a word is usually composed of at least one free morpheme. The bound morphemes that can be attached (before or after) to a free morpheme have rules for their sequencing. No changes can occur, for example, in the sequencing of the bound morphemes in the following words: *un-constitution-al-ity; ir-re-deem-able; happi-ness; pre-occupie-d.* Morphemes, their meanings, and their sequencing differ from language to language. In some languages, morphology plays a very major role.

The third component part of language form is *syntax*, which is a study of the arrangement of words in sentences. Word order plays a very big role in English compared to morphology. Notice, for example, how the order of words in the following sentences has a profound effect on their meanings:

> *The student greeted the teacher.*
> *The teacher greeted the student.*
> *She is a nurse.*
> *She is a good nurse.*
> *She is not a nurse.*
> *Is she a nurse?*
> *Only she is a nurse.*
> *She is only a nurse.*

The three component parts of language form — phonology, morphology, and syntax — are interrelated. Phonology permeates morphology and syntax; morphology permeates syntax; one sound can be a morpheme; and one morpheme can form a sentence. The interrelationship of these component parts is profound and intricate.

3. The Language Skills

The language skills are four: listening, speaking, reading, and writing. A closer look at these four skills reveals some insights which may have profound influence on teaching and learning styles and methodologies. It might be helpful to see a list of the four skills arranged this way:

        a. listening
        b. speaking
        c. reading
        d. writing

The first striking point about these skills is that the above arrangement follows the order in which the skills are naturally learned. A child learning her/his first language goes through these four stages in that order.

Secondly, the first two skills (listening and speaking) are the natural stages for language learning which apply even to illiterate persons. The last two skills (reading and writing) represent slightly later developments.

Thirdly, it is interesting to note that the first two skills (listening and speaking), which are often referred to as the aural-oral skills, represent both a receptive (listening) activity and a productive (speaking) activity. Naturally, any reaction, response, or interaction involved in listening is, in a way, productive; but as far as the intake is concerned, it is essentially a receptive activity. It is equally interesting to see that this receptive-productive element is also a feature of the last two skills (reading and writing), reading, of course, representing the receptive activity.   Just as in the case of listening, there is an element of productivity involved in any response to, or interaction with, the read passage. Additionally, there is another element of productivity involved in reading aloud.

Finally, in the process of language learning, it is of significance to note that, looking at the four skills backwards (or from the bottom up), it would not be difficult to realize that writing anything would be much easier if one has read it and seen it first, that reading anything (aloud) would be much easier if one has spoken it first, and that uttering anything would be much easier if one has heard it first. In other words, the four skills — in the process of language learning — are dependent upon each other in that order.

Perhaps an additional remark related to the skills would be appropriate at this point. A distinction should be made between listening (the first skill) and hearing. One might listen (even quite carefully) and not hear what is supposed to be heard. Particularly is this true in learning a second or foreign language. The fact is that native speakers of any language hear only the contrastive sound features (the phonemes) in their own language. They do not naturally hear the non-contrastive, non-distinctive sound features (the phonetic varieties) in their own language that hit their eardrums. For example, native speakers of English do not naturally hear the non-contrastive varieties of the /k/ sound in the following words: *kit, comb, caught,* and *coup.* So, while listening is a basic language skill, it is still very important to make sure that students also *hear* the distinctive varieties of sound in the stream of speech, especially in the case of a second or foreign language.

4. The Use of Language

Learning the component parts of language (the contrastive phonological elements, a limited but growing vocabulary, the more commonly used bound morphemes, and the basic syntactic patterns) and learning the four language skills is tantamount to saying that the students have acquired a particular proficiency level in the *structural patterns* of the language, or that they have attained a certain level of *language competence* (*linguistic competence*). The command of linguistic units and structures, however, is no guarantee that learners are able to communicate adequately and effectively. In other words, linguistic competence does not guarantee *communicative competence.* Unless the learners are made to *use* the language they are learning functionally and in appropriate situations, they cannot be said to be competent in communication. The *use of language*, then, from a pragmatic point of view, means the ability to dip into one's reservoir of language forms and units and to pick out of those numerous forms what would, in a specific situation, be appropriate for communicating the notions, functions, feelings and/or attitudes desired. Examples of such notions, functions, feelings and attitudes would be:

> *notions:* thanks, apology, description, reporting, time, place, etc.
> *functions:* inquiry, invitations, requests, commands, etc.
> *feelings:* anger, happiness, annoyance, satisfaction, approval, etc.

attitudes: optimism, pessimism, positivism, negativism, etc. These are purposes for which language is used. In other words, we use language to communicate notions, functions, feelings, and attitudes. To acquire communicative competence is to learn when and where to use specific forms to elicit the intended meaning.

5. The Major Objectives of Teaching and Learning the Language Arts

In the broadest terms, the umbrella objective of teaching and learning the language arts is to have students become effective communicators. Effectiveness in communication, one must remember, involves a process of growth and development. This growth and development is both cognitive and behavioral. As such, the process of growth and development should mean cognitive growth and behavioral changes at the same time. The cognitive growth that is involved in the development of language competence is related both to expression (form) and to content (meaning). The behavioral change that is involved in the development of the same language competence is related both to expression (form) and to the communicative act itself. This means that a language learner is immersed in an operation that involves

a. learning something about the language and the way it functions,

b. learning the meanings of the various forms one hears, utters, reads, and writes,

c. learning to use the various forms in appropriate linguistic and extra-linguistic (social, cultural) contexts, and

d. learning how to correlate the language being learned with social behavior appropriately in specific situations.

Stated in other words, the major objectives of teaching and learning the language arts are:

a. to learn the various phonological, morphological, and syntactic forms of the language,

b. to learn the four skills of language (listening, speaking, reading, and writing),

c. to use the language forms in appropriate situations, and

d. to emphasize a process of interaction and discourse in both oral and written language. (Keen, 1992)

Put in still other words, the major objectives of teaching and learning the language arts are the development of language competence and communicative competence at the same time.

6. The Determination of the Methodology to be Employed

The consideration of the objectives is of paramount importance in the determination of the methodology to be employed. The methodology, obviously, is not an end in itself, but rather a vehicle, a venue, that facilitates the attainment of the objectives. If the methodology and the objectives can be in harmony — if they can be integrated well — then the process will be enhanced and the methodology will be rendered more effective. Three different approaches will be discussed here.

a. *The Structural Approach.* The main characteristics of this approach are the following:

- It believes that language is basically a system of structures.
- It believes that these structures apply mainly to phonology and grammar.
- It believes that the structures taught must be placed in their right linguistic and cultural contexts.
- It believes that the learning of vocabulary comes gradually as learners develop their language skills.
- It believes that the language skills to be learned are understanding speech (listening), speaking, reading, and writing. (Linguistic habits are to be formed in these areas.)

(For learners of a second or foreign language)

- It believes that the structures of the learner's native language must be compared and contrasted with the structures of the target language.
- It believes that such a contrastive analysis will tell us in advance about the linguistic problems that a native speaker of one language is going to face in learning the target language.
- It believes that textbooks may be prepared in any target language with a specific native language in mind.

The structural approach was the first practical approach to foreign language teaching based on modern linguistic science. Hundreds of books for teachers and students have been published which are based on this approach, following all or most of the characteristics mentioned above.

The main weakness of this approach is that when structures are given too much attention and time (as they are in several textbooks and hundreds of classrooms), much of the practical and functional use of language is lost sight of. Very often the structural drills given in class have little or no functional value.

b. *The Communicative Approach.* The communicative approach — which is sometimes called the *notional* or the *functional* approach depending on the emphasis or the purpose involved — is a recent approach, having had its beginnings in the 1970's. The idea here is to start with the content to be communicated; that is, to see what "notions" (ideas) a person wants to "communicate" or what "functions" she/he wishes to have performed.   After determining the notions to be communicated or the functions to be performed, one selects the language elements (vocabulary and grammar) that best serve the communication of such notions.   Examples of these functions and notions are: time, space, attitude, agreement, request, disagreement, delight, apology, denial, anger, satisfaction, care, objection, etc.

The strengths of the communicative approach lie in the following facts:

• Language is viewed as a live means of communication.
• Language use — actual, live, real — is given paramount significance.
• Language is used to communicate certain ideas or notions —
(1)   in a variety of situations (formal, informal, serious, playful, etc.) and
(2)   with a variety of people (elders, peers, bosses, casual acquaintances, intimate friends, etc.) — requiring different language forms and levels for effective results.
• The purposes for which language is used are given initial and primary significance; the language forms (vocabulary, structure, etc.) that serve these purposes are selected accordingly.

This approach is very practical in the sense that students learn language elements that they can immediately experience in use.   But if this approach is followed without enough attention to structural matters, foreign language learners may end up learning a few things that they can use without developing the necessary language skills.   Besides, teachers whose own command of the language is not very strong may find this approach very difficult to adopt and follow.

c. *The Whole Language Approach.* This is the most recent approach to language teaching and learning.   The main characteristics of this approach are the following:

• It believes in the integration of the component parts of language.   Pronunciation, vocabulary, and grammar (morphology and syntax) are viewed as making up a whole.

- It believes in the integration of the language skills. Listening, speaking, reading, and writing are handled together in such a way that they function as component parts of language use and in such a way that they strengthen each other. To read a passage, for example, and interact with it in a class discussion, and then write something about it is seen as a comprehensive way of dealing with a subject.
- It believes in dealing with themes. Any theme can then lend itself to a great variety of activities, all requiring some use of language in one form or another.
- It believes in using original literature for the theme under discussion or study. Original literature here is not limited in meaning to English literature (meaning essays, novels, poetry, and the like), but all the literature available that is relevant to the theme being studied.
- It believes in encouraging students to use the language without fear or inhibition. Insistence upon correct and appropriate standard language use can be postponed until students have developed some self-confidence and some fluency and facility in the language.
- It believes that, within the framework of the above points, the sky's the limit for original and innovative techniques that teachers and students can develop in and out of class to arrive at the desired end: more effective communication.

While the whole language approach has been rightfully acclaimed to be one of the most natural and exciting ways of teaching language, it still has weaknesses mainly in the following areas:

- Without a concentrated (though partial) effort to overcome some structural problems (in phonology, morphology, and syntax), certain areas related to language form may go unnoticed.
- Some structuring and planning would be required to ensure that a course of study includes — somewhere along the line — the opportunity for students to handle and express common notions, functions, feelings, and attitudes.
- If the teacher is a little too permissive in the beginning, the development of a desirable atmosphere of confidence may result in the parallel development of wrong language habits that would be most difficult to correct subsequently.

- Without adequate training and retraining, teachers can find themselves running around in circles trying to make whole language work in their classrooms.

7. Conclusion on the Methodologies to Be Employed

Since this is not a book on language teaching and learning, the approaches discussed above have been dealt with very briefly. Students and teachers interested in pursuing the subject are advised to read more detailed accounts of these approaches in other books.

It is important at this stage to say that no single approach is alone going to solve all the problems we face in language teaching. Some approaches are better (or can be used more successfully) than others, but all approaches have some weaknesses and some strengths.

In the opinion of the author, the best total approach is really a combination of elements from various approaches that would best fit a particular learning-teaching situation. Such a learning-teaching situation is one that includes a consideration of the students' level and ability, the teachers' skills in the language they are teaching and their ability in teaching, the size of the classes, the presence or absence of various teaching aids, the nature of the textbooks used, the amount and kind of English that the students are likely to hear or use in the community, and so on.

Recent experience has indicated that the following combination of elements from various approaches would be very practical and successful, given the right conditions for its application:
- to base the teaching on the communicative approach in a whole language framework,
- to pay great attention to the careful grading of words and grammatical patterns so that the teachers and students can use a functional method while the learners develop the language skills gradually,
- to contextualize (situationalize) the language being taught as much as possible,
- to provide adequate pre-service and in-service teacher training, retraining, and tooling in the whole language and communicative approaches to learning and teaching, and to use from other approaches whatever elements seem to be useful and needed such as: reading (for specific purposes), explaining grammatical structures (where this answers a need), dictation (for the improvement of comprehension and spelling), various

writing exercises (to develop the skills of penmanship, vocabulary use, sentence construction, and theme development), a variety of teaching aids to facilitate the process of language learning (especially audio-lingual and computerized materials), and even translation (where this can save time and serve an immediate purpose with foreign learners).

8. Whole Education and the Language Arts

It is amply clear that the language arts aim at making students linguistically and communicatively more competent. Within a whole language framework and approach, there is the added advantage of integrating the component parts of language (phonology, morphology, and syntax), integrating the four language skills (listening, speaking, reading, and writing), and using language in as natural a way as possible, dealing with a variety of themes that could cut across a good number of academic disciplines.

Whole education would want to go further. Whole education would take the whole package (operation) of the language arts referred to above and integrate it with the lives of the students at school and in the community. A few examples will illustrate the point. (See Gillis, 1991)

a. *A Bulletin Board.* This can be quite an interesting activity with weekly news items from a variety of classes as well as from the community; with word and language puzzles; with announcements about essay competitions and debates; with funny anecdotes that actually took place at school or in the community; etc.

b. *A Newsletter.* This is a practical vehicle for recognizing language and artistic talent. Producing a weekly or monthly newsletter can follow a number of procedures that would not only develop the students' language and communication abilities, but also enhance their knowledge and skills in many other areas. An editorial board would develop parliamentary procedure skills, evaluation strategies, editorial skills, human relations, and the ability to meet deadlines.

c. *The Celebration of Birthdays.* Once every term, students can celebrate the birthdays of students falling during the term. Each time a different activity or theme can be followed. For example, on one occasion, some students may do the invitation cards; others may prepare cakes and cookies themselves and share the recipes with their classmates; and still others may be responsible for singing a song; etc. On another occasion, a particular theme or motto can be picked for each birthday student and developed in class by a classmate. The theme can emphasize the particular talents of the student or show some resemblance between the student and some important figure in history.

d. *Other Disciplines as Literature.* This can be a very fascinating activity. Students can be asked to bring to class certain passages from their textbooks (science, history, etc.) or from library books to show how these passages can be regarded as good literature for their style and development. Similar activities can be held in class dealing with newspaper or magazine articles as well as with speeches given in the community or in the country by local or national leaders.

e. *Community Activities.* This can be a very rewarding experience. Different students, according to their interests, can visit newspaper or magazine offices, printing presses, book publishing establishments, advertising agencies, or theater halls and, after observing their operations and interviewing a responsible person there, report (orally or in writing) on the visit — not only to enumerate the various activities (camera-like), but to react to, and interact with, the operation in such a way as to mention likes and dislikes, the contributions that these establishments make to the language arts and to the community, and how one might be able to learn from them and participate in some of their activities.

f. *Play Production.* This can be one of the richest and most exhilarating experiences ever. But to make it so, one should go beyond the traditional school play performances. If, after reading a number of short plays and examining their themes, characters, plots, sequences, and style, students can decide (in a class) on a live social issue for a theme, decide on the plot, design their characters and sequence of events, and write the play themselves, they will have a creative piece of work that the community will enjoy and support. Additionally, if the students in the art (design, or home economics) classes can prepare the costumes and set the stage with its various props, they will be integrating the artistic and technical angles in the activity. Also, if the students can design their own tickets and invitation cards, sell them in the community, and budget their expenses so that they will have some money left over for a worthy community project, then they will have rounded their activities and experiences and made them comprehensive and meaningful.

These are but a few examples, but they do illustrate the scope and dimensions that whole education would have in a particular discipline like the language arts.

Chapter Seven

Whole Education and the Social Sciences

1. What Are the Social Sciences?

It is sometimes not very easy to classify disciplines. Once a framework is prescribed, however, the task becomes infinitely easier. If we say that the social sciences include the disciplines that, in one way or another, relate to human behavior, then it would be little more than routine to classify sociology, history, economics, psychology, and political science as social sciences. What about language, though? Where would we classify language or linguistics? Well, linguistics is one of those unique sciences, because it can legitimately fall under a number of umbrellas. It can be classified under a physiological science with respect to the vocal apparatus that produces sounds; it can also be classified under a physical science with respect to sound waves and its acoustical nature; and it can be classified as a social science with respect to the communicative element involved.

Why are they called *social* sciences? Anything becomes social in nature when it relates to two or more persons. All the social sciences deal with human behavior. This is not news; it has been known for a very long time; mentioning it here is done for a very profound purpose that seems to have been lost in the quagmire. But first let us ask another question: Why are they called social *sciences*? They are sciences because of the methodology applied in studying them. The methodology is objective, rigorous, meticulous, and, in time, self-corrective. But because the social sciences are different in nature from the life and physical sciences, different social scientists, using the same objective methodology, can conceivably arrive at different conclusions. Nevertheless, it is the rigor in the methodology employed that makes those disciplines sciences (albeit of a social nature). Here again this is not news, but mentioning it has some underlying significance, especially in conjunction with the social nature of the disciplines.

Often what is covered and the way it is covered in some social science classes result in the loss of the most vital single element involved in teaching the social sciences, namely the balance between a behavioral approach to a subject (which may entail subjective and emotive judgments) and a scientific approach to the same subject (which should entail objective and detached judgments). The social sciences are not to be viewed just as subject-matter areas to be learned as information. The social sciences offer an invaluable opportunity for students to look at all aspects of human behavior scientifically, while at the same time retaining their own feelings and reactions to them. Maintaining this balance in the study of the social sciences helps in the development of individual personalities who can interact meaningfully with others and with life issues in the community.

2. The Major Objectives of Teaching and Learning the Social Sciences

The importance of the objectives (immediate, proximate, and ultimate) of any course of study can never be overemphasized. And keeping them in mind constantly as curricula are being designed and as methodologies are being planned can give needed focus and direction to the educative operation and process. In all courses of study — and particularly in the social studies — these objectives will not only determine and yield curricular activities and educational methodologies, but will also act as standard bearers for evaluation and assessment purposes. It is against these objectives that one can determine student progress and measure student growth and success. What, then, are the major objectives of teaching the social sciences in high school?

a. *Students will see themselves as products of several factors.* Students will see themselves as products of history and a part of it; they will see themselves as products of hereditary factors; they will see themselves as products of environmental (social and natural) factors; and they will see themselves as products of the interactions (with people and things) of which they are a part.

b. *Students will see themselves as contributors to the factors around them.* When students are limited to the role of observers (of events and proceedings), they will always feel aloof and detached; events lose their relevance as far as they are concerned. When they become active participants in the events around them, they take a much greater interest in them. When they influence events and are influenced by events at the same time, things assume a different perspective; life somehow becomes more alive, more dynamic, more relevant.

c. *Students will develop a wholesome self-concept.* Partly as a result of the first two objectives, students will develop a wholesome self-concept or self-image. This self-image is perhaps the greatest single factor contributing to a student's total well-being and to a student's value to others.

d. *Students will learn to be active participants in their communities as citizens.* The social studies can be a major venue for bringing this about. Students are not to view themselves as observers of civic events; they must participate actively in civic affairs.

e. *Students will see themselves as responsible participants in a democratic society.* One of the reasons why people rebel against any feature of society is that they see themselves as outsiders to the system. There has been too much talk and emphasis on rights and privileges without a commensurate insistence on responsibility to balance the rights. This responsibility should manifest itself in mutual respect and in sharing, at least on the social and intellectual levels. Each student must see herself/himself as a significant thread in the democratic fabric of society. (See Sigel and Hoskin, 1991)

f. *Students will see themselves as cementing factors in a culturally and ethnically diverse society.* There is a dual role to be played here. While students are to develop their self-concept and assume some pride (not false) in their ethnic and cultural backgrounds, they should, nevertheless, exhibit traits of cooperation, understanding, and sharing that will cement the diverse backgrounds and weave these heterogeneous elements into a united social fabric with common national goals and aspirations.

g. *Students will develop a broad perspective and see themselves as part of a world culture.* In the dynamic world of today, there is no room for isolationism. Every major event in any part of the world affects practically every other part. Besides, people and nations need each other. An understanding of other people and cultures is a key to successful global life and peaceful coexistence.

h. *Students will develop their knowledge, skills, attitudes, and emotions in a qualitative and balanced manner.* The development of knowledge entails the acquisition of information and understanding. The development of skills entails the ability to think rationally and to gather the information, analyze it, and use it, as well as the ability to communicate (receptively and productively). The development of attitudes entails the acquisition and application of positive and constructive dispositions to people, things, and events. The development of emotions entails the nurture and control of feelings that can color personal and interpersonal behavior.

i. *Students will develop the ability to make friends and widen their social horizons.* Learning to act, react, and interact in a positive, meaningful, and wholesome fashion is a key to making friends. Because "no man is an island", it is essential for students to learn to make friends and widen their social horizons. This, in a sense, is also a skill, but listing it separately is warranted because of its significance.

3. Integrating the Social Sciences

The commonest social science courses offered in high school are history (with a smattering of geography and politics) and economics (with a smattering of business studies). Whether the history is state history, regional history, U.S. history, or world history, the textbooks usually emphasize dates, incidents, and a progression of events. Occasionally matters related to government, politics, and geography seep into the picture. The causes and conditions precipitating such events as wars are mentioned and discussed. In economics courses, texts deal with the factors of production, supply and demand, business institutions, banking, markets, advertising, business and trade, and, very seldom, international transactions. Such courses, in their make-up are designed to operate like introductions to more in-depth collegiate counterparts. In college, however, two factors contribute to making them more relevant: the depth involved and the initial interest and motivation of students. In high school, these courses have a tendency to fall flat.

If the objectives of teaching and learning the social sciences are taken seriously, a concerted effort is expected of all the teachers involved in the social sciences to organize the course content and plan the strategies in methodology with a view to obtaining the desired outcomes in a very practical fashion. In terms of the social science course content, a major overhaul is needed to bring about a meaningful integration of the social sciences. One way (and certainly not the only way) to do this is to develop a number of themes in a historical perspective. The themes may include (for a course on the U.S.A.) (a) the struggle for independence; (b) the causes, process, and outcomes of the wars on American soil; (c) social and economic conditions from the days of the early settlements to 1779; (d) the impact of immigrants socially, economically, and culturally since 1779; (e) the development of political parties in the U.S.; (f) the life, struggles, and conditions of native Americans; (g) the life, struggles, and impact of Afro-Americans (h) the involvement of the U.S. in wars abroad; (i) the U.S. and the U.N. since 1949; (j) the changes in urban and rural living in the U.S. since 1900; (k) city, county, state, and federal governments; (l) the development of the electoral system; (m) the major social and economic problems since 1900; (n) the Constitution and Amendments; (o) minorities, their rights, and their responsibilities; (p) the development of industries in the U.S.; (q) U.S. imports, exports, and world markets; etc.

In terms of methodology, the strategy should include, whenever possible, a cross-section of effects and impacts. In other words, any event or situation or condition should be seen from a human, social, economic, political, and psychological angle if this can add pertinence and relevance to the subject. Personal reactions and interactions should be allowed and encouraged. Class discussions, oral and written reports, and other activities can be geared to fostering a better understanding of the topics and themes as well as a personal involvement and interaction in the process. When the social sciences are handled this way, and when the objectives listed above are consciously in the planning of the course content and methodological strategies, the students will live the issues, sensing their impact and examining ways of impacting them themselves.

4. Integrating the Social Sciences With Other Disciplines

A number of objectives (major and minor) in various disciplines can be undermined if the work done by different teachers is not properly integrated. For example, if the history teacher does not insist on the same language standards required by the English teacher, much of the students' efforts can be lost, and so can much of the needed reinforcement. But this is not the only kind of integration desired. In looking for themes to develop debates, oral reports, written reports, and essays, why can't the English teacher use some of the social-science-related themes as a base? Further, why can't the art teacher — if only for emphasis — point out some trends, motifs, and styles that belonged to different times and eras studied in the social science curriculum? Similarly, why can't the social science teacher bring out a number of science-related or art-related facts belonging to different periods under study in the social science class? If the details of the various course curricula are known to all the teachers of the same grade level — and especially if an effort is made by the teachers of various subjects to inject integrative elements into their own curriculum — then much of the desired outcomes (interrelationship, impact, wholeness, relevance, meaningfulness, etc.) can be realized.

This kind of integration can be brought about very effectively through some extra-class activities. A visit to a history museum, for example, would be an excellent and meaningful venue for seeing the interrelationship of the arts, the language arts, and the social sciences. A visit to a science museum or a zoo can be an equally good venue to relate the arts, the sciences, and the social sciences. An in-class or extra-class activity that can be extremely stimulating is to take an idea, a notion, or a theme (such as war, love, nature, relations, fury, God, faith, serenity, excitement, hope, patriotism, space, etc.) and see how it is manifested in literature (prose or poetry), music, art (paintings, sculpture, ceramics), politics, history, science, and the community. This can effectively integrate the language arts, the humanities, the sciences, and the social sciences. All it takes is a little vision, seriousness in implementing the concept, and team work to execute it. It will not happen automatically or by accident. It needs be planned curricularly and methodologically, and the results will show a world of difference in both the quality of the work performed by students and by the change of attitude to something more positive, more dynamic, and more relevant.

5. Whole Education and the Social Sciences

The very nature of the social sciences is such that it can encompass a wide variety of activities and experiences to help make the subject(s) come alive. Whole education looks with seriousness and determination at the major objectives of teaching and learning the social sciences and devises ways and means (in school and in the community) to ensure their realization. Key concepts in this connection are *interaction* and *involvement*. To bring these about, three ingredients are necessary:

thought-provoking activities, active participation in a number of endeavors, and real experiences in democratic living.

Towards this end, a few suggestions are made; they are not exhaustive; they are meant only as samples to illustrate the scope that the social sciences should have within a whole education framework.

a. *Visits to community centers, institutions and associations.* These can be real eye-openers concerning the work that different segments of the community are undertaking. They would include the police headquarters, the fire department, municipal offices, the Department of Motor Vehicles, old people's homes, recreational centers, institutions and schools for the disabled, tourist agencies, information centers, etc.

b. *Reading books and novels and/or watching movies or plays dealing with war.* These might include *All Quiet on the Western Front, Three Soldiers, Miss Saigon, To Hell and Back, Welcome Home,* and many others.

c. *Understanding the meaning of the celebrated holidays.* These would include Independence Day, Thanksgiving, Martin Luther King's Birthday, Presidents' Birthday, St. Patrick's Day, religious holidays, Memorial Day, Mother's Day, Armed Forces Day, Flag Day, Father's Day, Labor Day, etc.

d. *Correspondence with pen pals.* This can be done internationally with an exchange of information about habits, traditions, cultural elements, foods, sports, education, economic and political systems, dress, industries, climate, etc.

e. *Featuring ethnic minorities.* This could be an in-class, a school, or a community activity with a display of native costumes, artifacts, and music, as well as a sampling of the native foods and perhaps translations of the ethnic literature.

f. *Welcoming foreign visitors in class.* These visits by foreigners (students, tourists, businessmen, educators, diplomats, etc.) can be very interesting and stimulating, especially if they include discussions on political, social, religious, and economic issues.

g. *Welcoming civil servants in class.* This brings a part of the community into the classroom. Students have a chance to ask personal questions about the functioning of the civic mechanism in their area. If the school happens to be in or near a capital city, dignitaries from the local or federal government may make occasional visits, too.

These and other similar activities supplement and reinforce the basic knowledge elements of a social science course.

Additionally,

• they get the students involved in different aspects of the social, cultural, and political life around them;

• they help students gain an understanding of other peoples and cultures;

• they help students overcome their biases and prejudices;

• they help develop interrelationships and friendships;

• they make life in the community more dynamic and relevant;

• they help develop tolerance and compassion; and

• they help students assume more responsible roles in a democratic society.

Chapter Eight

Whole Education and the Life and Physical Sciences

1. What Are the Life and Physical Sciences?

The life sciences are the systematic studies of animates or living organisms and creatures. These are generally divided into two branches: animals and plants. The sciences that deal with specific areas of animal and plant life are the following: *anatomy* (which deals with human and animal bodies), *physiology* (which deals with how living bodies function), *biology* (which deals with all living organisms), *zoology* (which deals with all kinds of animals), and *botany* (which deals with plants).

The physical sciences are the systematic studies of animates or non-living elements that have a material existence — i.e., that exist in the form of matter (in motion) . These sciences include the following: *chemistry* (which deals with all the substances or elements which make up living or non-living things), *physics* (which deals with all matter and the forces in nature such as motion, light, and heat), *geology* (which deals with the elements found in the earth such as soil, rock, and layers thereof), *astronomy* (which deals with all celestial bodies and their movements), and *meteorology* (which deals with atmospheric conditions and the weather).

Additionally, there are some sciences that integrate the studies of two or more of the physical sciences. These include such areas as *astrophysics* (which deals with the chemical nature of celestial bodies), and *geophysics* (which deals with the movements of different parts of the earth). There are also some other sciences that cut across the life and physical sciences in some integrative way. These include such an area as *bio-chemistry* (which deals with the chemistry of living organisms).

It is interesting to note at this point that there are areas of study that cut across the social sciences and the life and physical sciences in a fascinatingly integrative fashion. These include such areas as *ecology* (which deals with the interrelationship of humans, animals, and plants with each other and with their environment), *physical anthropology* (which deals with human nature, race, and physical form compared with the nature and forms of animals), and *geo-politics* (which deals with the influence of a country's location and population on its politics).

2. The Major Objectives of Teaching and Learning the Sciences

It is one thing to have a list of objectives on paper and a very different thing to make these objectives impact upon the content and methodology of a course or courses of study. Whole education insists upon making every agreed upon objective a vital guide for, and a strict determiner of, content details and methodological procedures. It is with this view in mind that the following major objectives of teaching and learning the sciences are given.

a. *Students will develop skills in thinking scientifically.* This is easier said than done. It cannot happen over-night. It is a thinking process that takes time and practice. Scientific thinking involves a number of activities and sub-skills, chief among which are the following:

- learning to focus on a single problem at a time,
- learning to eliminate irrelevant and unrelated factors and variables,
- learning to collect useful and pertinent information (and discard irrelevant material),
- learning to classify the information collected under designated categories,
- learning to analyze the information,
- learning to guess at, think out, or postulate possible solutions,
- learning to arrange the possible solutions in order of best anticipated results,
- learning to try out and experiment with one solution at a time (trial-and-error experience),
- learning to verify results,
- learning to make generalizations and come to conclusions,
- learning to edit, revise, and reexamine the data and the

conclusions, and
  • learning to apply the results.
  b. *Students will learn to think objectively.* Very much as a result of learning the steps above, students will develop a detached (objective) disposition to the handling of data and solutions.
  c. *Students will orient themselves to their animate and inanimate surroundings.* Understanding one's environment and how it functions is a significant step towards the control and the conservation of the environment.
  d. *Students will interact with their environment.* It is important for students to interact with the living and nonliving elements in their environment on the basis of understanding.
  e. *Students will develop an affinity with the natural world around them.* It is equally important to have a direct and meaningful relationship between an individual and certain aspects or manifestations of the natural world (both animate and inanimate).
  f. *Students will see how the various sciences are integrated together.* This integration is not limited to the method of approach (the scientific method), but it touches upon the very content of the sciences themselves: the way they are related to each other, the way they influence each other, and the way in which certain laws or conditions affect them in similar ways.
  g. *Students will learn to integrate scientific knowledge with other knowledge.* This is part of the overall objective of curricular integration. More will be said about this below.
  h. *Students will learn to integrate the sciences and the curriculum as a whole with life in the community.* This will also be dealt with subsequently.
  i. *Students will develop an appreciation of nature as well as a positive attitude towards it.*
  j. *Students will love their natural environment and care for it.*

An examination of these ten objectives will clearly show that the first three (a through c) help develop what is often referred to as intellectual discipline. The next five objectives (d through h) develop relevant integrative and interactive skills. The last two objectives (i and j) deal with the affective nature of students and help develop wholesome feelings towards the natural environment and world about us. Put together, these objectives constitute an integrated whole in our approach to the sciences which are not only growing in depth and scope themselves, but which are exerting an ever-increasing influence and impact on our daily lives.

3. Integrating the Life and Physical Sciences

There are several reasons why the life and physical sciences need to be taught and learned in an integrated way, chief among which are the following:

a. *All of them deal with the natural world.* They all fall under the same umbrella. Important relationships can be lost sight of if the life and physical sciences are constantly and consistently being departmentalized and compartmentalized.

b. *The scientific method applies to all of them.* All the life and physical sciences are approached and studied in essentially the same way.

c. *There is a profound relationship among the life sciences.* This is not only because they all deal with living organisms, but because these organisms have much in common, and they are influenced by outside factors in much the same way.

d. *There is a profound relationship among the physical sciences.* The laws that govern matter and motion permeate practically all the physical sciences.

e. *There is a dynamic relationship between the life sciences and the physical sciences.* All living organisms have a chemical make-up. Practically all the elements in physical nature (oxygen, nitrogen, motion, gravity, electricity, geography, meteorology, etc.) have a profound effect on living organisms; and the opposite is also true: living organisms of all kinds have a great effect on the physical environment.

f. *Many of the concepts learned (categories, relationships, order, system, etc.) can be seen more dynamically and more effectively if an integrated approach is followed in studying the life and physical sciences.* Educators emphasize the importance of problem solving as an effective method of learning. This needs to be matched by equally effective materials (textbooks, manuals, etc.) and equally effective classroom methodologies to make it a reality. How much more successful it would be to have students draw from a variety of the sciences at the same time in solving problems dealing with machines, cars, aviation, appliances, electricity, pollution, disease, poisoning, first aid techniques, marine life, sports, diets, health, and the like.

4. Integrating the Sciences With Other Disciplines

There is nothing like seeing life as a whole. This is the way people see things in their proper perspective and in their proper relationships. The examples given here are meant only to illustrate how easily the life and physical sciences can be integrated with other disciplines for better performance in all the disciplines as well as for a more wholesome approach to life and education.

a. *The sciences and the language arts.* Obviously, every discussion on a science topic requires verbal and/or written expression. This is hardly the point. More important are the following considerations:

• How are the standards required in the language course made to bear on what is expressed (verbally or in writing) in the science class?

• How can a rigorous, detached, objective, precise approach to scientific subjects influence students' writing styles?

• How can a scientific theme be dealt with creatively in a language class?

• How can the terminology acquired in the science class be used actively to expand the students' language vocabulary?

• How can techniques of note-taking, summarizing, paraphrasing, reporting, scanning, etc., be used effectively in the science class?

b. *The sciences and the social sciences.* In dealing practically with natural disasters such as earthquakes, floods, and hurricanes, wouldn't an integrated approach covering geography, ecology, economics, social behavior, water supply, medical facilities, housing, transportation, education, politics, and the like be instrumental in understanding and solving the problems at hand? For another example, wouldn't a thorough knowledge of technology contribute to the understanding of economic problems, war outcomes, and standards of living?

c. *The sciences and the arts.* Wouldn't students' lives be more interesting and challenging if some of the sciences (e.g., chemistry, metallurgy, physics, etc.) come in handy when doing pieces of art work (e.g., painting, sculpture, pottery, ceramics, and the like)?
Conversely, wouldn't a significant esthetic element be added if what is learned in the arts and crafts class can be at least partially used or applied in science reports, scientific experiments, and science exhibits?

d. *The sciences and physical education.* This is a very practical sphere where the interplay is a necessity. Anyone interested in sports and physical education — even in the remotest way — should find herself/himself motivated enough to learn about diets, physiology, medications, etc.

The sciences are related to each other and, in a very real and meaningful way, they are related to other disciplines. A concerted effort is needed to see that the vital relationships among the various disciplines are brought out in the curricular content and the educational methodology to make their study relevant, interesting, exciting, and practical. The teachers who can be very successful doing this are ones who are experts in one field and who have avocational interests in other areas.

One practical way of bringing this about is to use computer-generated programs in the classrooms. Several of these include an inter-disciplinary approach to the sciences and to related areas of life. Going through such programs, the students get much more involved in the subjects, they actually do things (on the computer) and see relationships and consequences, and they see the sciences as integral parts of their life experiences.

Another example of an inter-disciplinary approach, with science as the base, is to take a theme such as *cars* and deal with it in terms of the following bases:

- the engine (touching upon mechanics, electricity, energy, motion, weight, etc.),
- the design and interior (touching upon design, shape, colors, art, fabric, paint, etc.),
- purchase and finance (touching upon cost, economics, banks, loans, interest, insurance, etc.),
- traffic rules and regulations (touching upon civic responsibility, courtesy, etc.), and
- transportation (touching upon service, car pools, other means, pollution, etc.).

If the focal point in the science class is mechanics (in physics), the car theme can bring this about in a relevant and wholesome and exciting way for students. But this needs a concerted effort on the part of educational planners, textbook authors, and teachers.

5. Whole Education and the Life and Physical Sciences

Whole education makes education relevant to the life of each individual student. If we are to give practical meaning to the maxim that "education is life", we must make certain that the subject matter in education both *comes* (emanates) from life situations and conditions and also *relates* immediately back to life situations and conditions. The extent to which school subjects do not emanate from life and are not related meaningfully to it is the measure of the relevance gap in education today.

The example of the car theme given above may be expanded and applied to the community. If there happens to be a local industry (cars, machinery, spare parts, textile, agricultural, etc.) the schools and the community can share in the benefits of student visits to such industries. The visits, obviously, should not be reduced to touristic ones; they should involve the students in a thorough understanding of the workings of the industry in a complete cycle including the following: where the primary products came from (production, source) and how (transportation, purchase, importation, tariffs, cost, financing, etc.), the detailed process of production (assembly line, machines and how they work, ingredients, additives, design, final product, packaging, etc.), economic considerations (consumption, export, sales, demand, supply, employment, etc.), and the history of the industry and the prospects of its development. The mutual benefits of an approach of this nature are enormous. For the students, it is basically a matter of seeing how academic subjects like physics, chemistry, economics, history, and human relations are functionally at work in the community. Additionally, the exposure itself may open up vistas of interest in a variety of areas of future employment and/or specialization. For the industry, the development of community awareness and moral support is exceedingly beneficial. In addition, from among the students, there is a real possibility of present and future part-time or full-time employment.

The above examples only illustrate the infinite possibilities that the community can provide to augment, reinforce, and integrate what is academically constructed in the schools. (See Yager, 1993)

One last point is worth mentioning and emphasizing here. Earlier on, mention was made of having the teachers add the affective element of caring into their teaching. It is equally important for teachers to develop the affective caring element in their students. In the study of the various sciences, if somehow students can be made to love nature and various aspects of it (animals, birds, plants, mountains, rivers, sunsets, moon-lit nights, natural laws, etc.), they will yearn to learn more about them and develop a desire to care for and conserve them.

That in itself can be the greatest motivating factor to further study. And when this is coupled with the relevance element involved in integrating academic knowledge with life situations and conditions, learning can be at its best and achievement can soar immeasurably.

Chapter Nine

Whole Education and Mathematics

1. Introduction

There is no escape from mathematics. Whichever way a person turns, she/he would need some form of mathematics to get by. The Chinese and other Far Eastern civilizations realized this fact over five thousand years ago and devised the abacus to help them do their calculations. The Greek philosophers went further when they stated over two thousand years ago that mathematics would be good for training the mind. Dealing with numbers and figures, it is true, sharpens the mind. But this sharpening of the mind is not an end in itself; it can have practical, transfer value that can help in the solution of many everyday problems. To think exactly, to think accurately, to think meticulously, to think logically, and to solve problems by having one's mind move methodically from step to step are some of the practical benefits of studying mathematics.

Nobody denies that, but the pressing problem at hand is how the study of mathematics is to be packaged for high school purposes. This has been a lingering question with no adequate solution. The teaching of mathematics has been extremely traditional in the way it has been packaged: departmentalized specializations in miniature spanning the high school years. The study of mathematics has been truly "academic" with little (and, in some cases, no) relevance to life.

Something needs to be done about that. It is not just a matter of updating the methodology and techniques of classroom teaching. It is a matter of redesigning the content of mathematics courses and applying appropriate methodologies that will spell the saving grace. The aim should be a better quality and higher standards of performance by teachers and students alike. Textbook authors, too, should rethink and redesign their contents. Curriculum designers should demand it.

2. The Major Objectives of Teaching and Learning Mathematics

It is the students who raise the *why* question about certain mathematics courses, and it is usually very seriously asked. Somehow the basic purposes of different mathematics courses have not been clarified to students at the outset. Perhaps even some teachers get so involved with their "courses" that they often lose sight of the fundamental reasons for teaching mathematics in high school. The major objectives of teaching and learning mathematics are the following:

a. *Students will become familiar and comfortable with the worlds of numbers and quantity.* There is no escape in real life from the fact that we need to deal with numbers and quantity practically continuously. The *how much* segment of our daily experience is enormous, and those who feel uncomfortable with it and balk at handling it find themselves greatly handicapped and disadvantaged. Many of those who do feel uncomfortable with numbers and quantity are ones who resorted to technological aids (such as calculators) before developing the necessary and essential skills to make numbers and quantity matters of second nature.

b. *Students will learn to think logically.* It has been said that common sense is not very common. Unfortunately, we can probably add that logical thinking does not fare much better. Learning to think logically is a process of development that requires both practice and time. In mathematics, logical thinking is applied to numbers, quantity, shapes, sequences, and processes, and it has enormous transfer value to numerous kinds of life situations.

c. *Students will learn to see relationships.* This involves comparisons and contrasts, as well as ratios. Viewing things in perspective — which entails seeing similarities, differences, and relative values — is greatly enhanced by various branches of mathematics.

d. *Students will learn to quantify concepts and bodies of information.* This is a receptive, as well as a productive, ability. To understand a figure and to be able to give a figure as a representation of an idea or a bit of information are essential skills in today's world.

e. *Students will learn problem solving.* Using a combination of the objectives mentioned above, students can attempt the solutions of a number of problems through mathematics if, somehow, the ingredients or elements involved in the problems are quantifiable. The transfer value of this skill is virtually unlimited in real life situations.

f. *Students will develop the skills of calculating, estimating, and making intelligent guesses.* Again using a combination of the above objectives, students can make mental calculations and estimations as well as intelligent guesses about sequences and results that would be greatly enhanced by the study of mathematics. This is why the use of calculators too early in the game can act like a crutch, stifling the development of the mental capacity to make such guesses and calculations.

g. *Students may be attracted to become future mathematicians and specialists in mathematics-related fields.* This is true of all fields, of course, but it is intentionally mentioned here for two reasons: it is obviously good to discover the talents of future mathematicians, physicists, astronomers, computer technicians, engineers, and the like; and it is equally important to realize that the other students in class (in most cases, the majority) may not end up in such fields, but are ones who still need to be motivated enough to go through a process that has such great transfer value in life. So many mathematics teachers miss the boat (in terms of essential objectives) by falsely assuming that all the students in class are automatically motivated enough to become engineers or mathematicians.

A number of examples will be given subsequently to illustrate the various points and objectives mentioned in this section.

3. Integrating the Study of Mathematics

The story I am about to relate may sound extreme to some readers; to others, however, it may illustrate a typical phenomenon. Not too long ago, I visited an algebra class with ninth, tenth, and eleventh graders in it. The student in front of me was obviously absent from class except for his body; he was not listening to what was going on in class; he was not participating in any way; he was busy reading a paperback throughout the class period. When I asked the teacher about him, he said, "Oh, that one! He's taking the course for the third time." When I remarked that he would probably fail it again the way he was behaving, the teacher's response was, "Well, students who fail it the third time take it in summer, and everyone passes in summer."

What kind of school standards, county standards, state standards, or national standards are we aiming for in a case like that? It does not take much to realize that algebra was not making a dent in this boy's life; it was utterly irrelevant to him. In his own mind, perhaps the following thoughts would fleet through: "Algebra? Quadratic equations? Unknowns? Numerators and denominators? What for?" The tragedy does not end here, though. What was the teacher doing for three years? What is the real philosophy of the school in this respect and what was it doing about it? Somehow it seemed as though everyone was just waiting for this student to get a passing mark (very undeservedly) in the summer session and move on, as if there was not even one iota of interest in having him attain some measure of the basic objectives mentioned above.

That algebra as such was of no particular interest to that student is not surprising. What is surprising and sad, however, is why and how the teacher and the school were making no attempt to show the majority of students (who are definitely not bent on becoming majors in mathematics-related areas) how relevant algebra and the other fields of mathematics (like arithmetic, geometry, and calculus) are to their everyday lives.

This in itself raises a fundamental question: On what basis is a course (any course, but, in this case, in mathematics) like algebra made a high school requirement? Perhaps two mathematics courses should be required of all students. The first should probably be titled something like "Life Mathematics" and should include elements of the following:

• bookkeeping essentials with journal entries and a ledger, debits and credits, and a profit-and-loss statement (involving no more than arithmetical computations),

• basic statistics, dealing with samples, numbers, ratios, means, medians, standard deviations, tables, and graphs,

• essentials of plane geometry, dealing with shapes, angles, lines, some axioms and postulates, a few basic theorems, and design,

• essentials of algebra, dealing with basic problem-solving experiences (such as ones dealing with rate, time, and distance), and

• exercises in logic, bringing a variety of the above to bear on the solution of problems.

This way, it is not difficult to surmise, the relevance of mathematics will be made very clear in a practical way for students. This would provide the mathematical basis for life operations that demand it. Everybody needs this basis to handle the most rudimentary tasks in life.

Education in school would be providing a nice academic framework for some of the skills required for the handling of everyday operations and experiences. The exposure of students to this academic framework in mathematics might in itself motivate some students to seek more in-depth courses.

The second requirement (which should be an elective out of a limited number) or a straight mathematics elective can provide more in-depth study and be a possible launching pad for future specialists in mathematics-related domains. On the high school level, this second course should, at least to some extent, be also related to life experiences.

4. Integrating Mathematics With Other Disciplines

Integration can be brought about if there is a concerted effort on the part of teachers to relate subjects together in a meaningful manner. Naturally, the sciences lend themselves very much to an integral relationship with mathematics. Astronomy, physics, chemistry, mechanics, and even physiology and biology have a relationship, and can be understood better, with mathematics as an adjunct. But this is not the extent of it. The study of the social sciences — especially economics and sociology — can be greatly enhanced by some mathematical skills. The point is this: Are the curriculum designers, the textbook authors, and the classroom teachers going to cooperate to bring about a meaningful and integrative approach to the study of various branches of knowledge?

If the physics teacher brings some of the elements taught in the mathematics class to bear on physics; if the social science teacher dealing with demographic elements brings tables and charts and graphs to bear on the social science lesson; if the economics teacher dealing with banks and money and budget and supply and demand can bring mathematical computations in to clarify concepts and transactions; if the mathematics teacher (in the "Life Mathematics" course) can draw from those other disciplines certain elements and problems that can be solved or analyzed or understood better in the mathematics class; then there will be a dynamic academic intercourse that cuts across disciplines to be handled in a holistic fashion. This is what life is about. This is what education should be about. This is what whole education is about.

Following are a few examples (definitely not exhaustive) to illustrate the nature of an integrative, inter-disciplinary approach to mathematics:

a. *Integration with the sciences.* This is where there is a very natural relationship. With a bit of planning and effort, a number of students can come alive this way.

- The various means of communication and travel (planes, trains, ships, and cars) can provide scientific knowledge of different types (locomotives, engines, lift, gravity, electricity, etc.) and a number of significant mathematical computations: time-rate-distance problems; conversion of pounds to kilograms, dollars to a variety of other currencies, Centigrade to Fahrenheit temperatures, and miles to kilometers; specific gravities; freight volume measurements; and so on.

- Similarly, any aspect of astronomy and geology may have numerous mathematical and statistical computations appended.

- The study of different elements in physics (pulleys, falling bodies, weight loss in liquids, temperatures, distances, weights, rocket curves in flight, etc.) will necessitate mathematical computations and calculations.

b. *Integration with the social sciences.* Again with some planning and coordination, mathematics can be brought to bear on different aspects of the social sciences to make them come alive in a very real and meaningful way for students.

- In the study of economics, students can use statistics, graphs, tables, and a number of mathematical and arithmetic computations and calculations to deal with elements of supply and demand, prices, interest rates, taxes, revenues, tariffs, profit and loss statements, exchange rates, and the like.

- In the study of sociology, which would include demographic features, statistics and graphs, students can use some calculations that would be required to better understand birth and death rates, immigration numbers and quotas, age groups, employment, welfare, and so on.

c. *Integration with other subjects.* Naturally, the sciences and the social sciences (in that order) lend themselves to mathematical considerations, but other subjects can also be enhanced by mathematics.

- Health and physical education classes can make use of a whole barrage of calculations (dealing with diets, calories, weights, disease, and track and field events) to turn them into real-life experiences.

- Art and music classes can also make use of mathematics (in matters dealing with pitch, frequency, tone, color, and design) and turn them into exciting experiences.

Integration means something very special. Most science classes have some mathematics in them; social science, health, physical education, arts, and music classes can have some mathematics injected into them, but this is hardly the point. It is *not* just a matter of *mixing in* different subjects. Integration means much more than that. It means bringing different disciplines to bear on each other in a meaningful, real-life fashion as a result of a concerted effort on the part of textbook authors, curriculum designers, educational administrators, and teachers to create a realistic, multi-faceted situation for students to experience.

5. The Development of Logic, Insight, and Creativity

No course or group of courses can ever claim monopoly over the teaching of logic, insight, and creativity. Logic does not *belong exclusively* to mathematics, any more than creativity belongs to art exclusively. All courses or emphases can teach logic or help in the development of insight or contribute towards the nurturing of creativity, but the very nature of a course may lend itself more, and make a bigger contribution, to the attainment of certain objectives.

In this respect, it is safe to say that one of the major objectives of teaching mathematics is the development of logic, not only to solve mathematical problems, but also for its transfer value in other areas of life. Logic, it may be added, is not unrelated to insight and creativity. As a matter of fact, all three of these enhance each other. Towards this end, here are just a few illustrations of how the three elements (logic, insight, and creativity) can be nurtured and developed in mathematics classes. (These are expressed mainly in the form of questions.)

• You have a blue marble and a red marble in your hand. Without looking, you roll them on the floor. What chance is there that the blue marble will come out first? (Answer: one out of two.)

• You add a green marble to the blue and red marbles. Now when you roll them on the floor, what chance is there that the blue marble will come out first? (Answer: one out of three.)

• If you roll these three marbles (blue, red, and green) on the floor again, what chance is there that they will come out in that order (blue first, then red, then green)? (Answer: one out of six. It may be good to ask students to chart all the possibilities to see why and how it is one out of six:

blue	blue	red	red	green	green
red	green	green	blue	blue	red
green	red	blue	green	red	blue

This way it becomes a reality.)

• You want to serve colorful, two-tone gelatin salads in clear-glass dishes. You can vary the top and bottom colors as often as you can with the lemon (yellow), lime (green), and cherry (red) gelatin. How many different combinations can you make? (Answer: six.)

| (top) | lime | lemon | lime | cherry | lemon | cherry |
| (bottom) | lemon | lime | cherry | lime | cherry | lemon |

(This has very practical application possibilities.)

• You have six people for dinner, including yourself. You ask them to sit wherever they please, in the six chairs around the rectangular dining table. What chance is there that the eldest person will be at the head of the table? (Answer: one out of six.)

• With the same group, if they are asked to sit wherever they please, what chance is there that the eldest person will be at the head of the table, and moving from his right, that the others will be seated in order of age (eldest to youngest) around the table? (Answer: one in 720. To arrive at this figure: it is one out of six for the eldest to be at the head; it is one out of five for the next eldest to be on his or her right; it is one out of four for the next one; and so on. Multiply $6 \times 5 \times 4 \times 3 \times 2 = 720$.)

• There are some birds on a tree and some on the ground. If one bird from the tree joins the birds on the ground, the number of birds on the tree will equal the number of birds on the ground. If one bird from the ground joins the birds on the tree, the birds on the tree will be twice as many as the ones on the ground. How many birds are on the tree and how many birds are on the ground now? (Answer: seven on the tree and five on the ground. Because one would logically assume that the numbers would have to be small, trial-and-error guessing is possible. When my father first gave me this riddle, I was a high school student. I promptly brought out a piece of paper and solved the problem algebraically:

Birds on the tree $= x$
Birds on the ground $= y$
$x - 1 = y + 1$; $x - y = 2$; $x = y + 2$
$x + 1 = 2(y-1)$; $x + 1 = 2y - 2$; $x - 2y = -3$
Substitute for x in the second equation:
$y + 2 - 2y = -3$; $-y = -5$; $y = 5$
Birds on the ground $= 5$
Birds on the tree $= y + 2 = 7$

This was the first practical benefit I derived from algebra!)

Note that the development of logical thinking in the solution of this problem includes:

. the realization that the difference in the numbers of birds in both groups is *two*, since by adding one bird to one group, the group will be equal in number,

. the realization that the numbers must be *small*, since the addition of one bird to the ones on the tree will *double* the ones on the ground, and

. the realization that the numbers should be *odd*, since adding *one* bird to one group will *double* the number in the other group.

- Fill the blanks in the following sets:
  - a. 1, 3, 5, 7, ___ (Answer: 9; add 2.)
  - b. 2, 5, 8, 11, ___ (Answer: 14; add 3.)
  - c. 3, 9, 27, 91, ___ (Answer: 243, multiply by 3.)
  - d. 1, 2, 4, 8, ___ (Answer: 16; double the 8.)
  - e. 1, 4, 9, 16, ___ (Answer: 25; squares of 1, 2, 3, 4,5.)
  - f. 1, 8, 27, 64, ___ (Answer: 125; cubes of 1, 2, 3, 4, 5.)

The above sets are relatively easy. To broaden the students' horizons and develop their creativity, other sets can be given like the following:
  - a. 1904, ..., 1992, ___ (Answer, 1996 = leap years.)
  - b. 4, 1, 1, 5, ___ (Answer: 3 = first Mondays of the first five months in 1993.) - *(Even if students do not guess this one, merely giving them such a possibility opens up huge vistas of imagination in their minds.)*

- The same idea can be applied to different shapes and geometric figures.

- Games are a fascinating and capturing means of developing logic, insight, and creativity. The social game of animate/inanimate or animal/mineral can sharpen the mind immeasurably. Other games like *Monopoly* and *Cluedo* can be very instrumental in this regard.

6. Whole Education and Mathematics

Mathematics is inescapable; it is part of our lives. If it is handled with its various branches in school as an integral part of our experience, students will see its relevance, and they will love it. But when it is isolated from real life, when all it purports to be is purely academic, students are alienated from it, and they tend to hate it. Whole education provides opportunities — real-life opportunities — for students to handle, play with, deal with, experience mathematics, on a variety of levels and in various domains, not only as a means of survival, but also, and more importantly, as a means of better quality living and, possibly, a means of stimulating vocational and professional outlets and interests.

Towards this end, whole education seeks to integrate the manifold facets of mathematics not only with other disciplines, as has been indicated earlier, but also with the community and the various enterprises in it. The following suggestions merely illustrate the almost unlimited wealth of resources available in the community, partly to augment the academic side of mathematics learning and partly to let students experience the value and use of mathematics in their daily lives.

• Visits to banks and money exchange stations would be an unforgettable experience, especially if there is someone there to show the students a bit of interest and to give them first-hand knowledge about how these institutions work by showing them real transactions.

• Visits to travel offices and agencies (or airlines) would be eye-openers with respect to travel costs (and discounts), high season and low season differences, group rates, distances, tour and group packages (and their implications), baggage allowances, reservations, hotel accommodations, etc.

• Visits to accounting and tax offices are necessary experiences to have the philosophy and procedures explained.

• Visits to industrial establishments would work wonders with students when they study production techniques and assembly lines, when they see employees at work, when they are told about salaries and benefits, and when they appreciate the costs and labor that go into the finished products.

• Visits to farms would not only develop in students the respect they should have for farmers and rural life, but would also make them understand how farms contribute to the economic life of a nation. This could become a very meaningful experience as the students go through some typical activities involving budgets, production, and marketing related to a farm and its products.

If these and other similar experiences can be integrated with work done in the mathematics class (such as preparing a particular budget for a firm, doing a tax return for a real or hypothetical business, calculating all costs involved in a group trip on the basis of limited individual budgets, working out a profit-and-loss statement on the basis of given journal entries, and the like) by having the teacher assign tasks and projects (on the basis of individual or group interest), then different aspects of mathematics can have real meaning to students.

The same idea, of course, can apply in geometry if the visits are made to architectural offices where designs are prepared. They can also apply in algebra and calculus if the visits are made to astronomical observatories or space stations. The idea is hopefully amply clear: as an integral part of life, mathematics must be seen by students as a very real and relevant and necessary knowledge and skill.

Chapter Ten

Whole Education and the Liberal Arts

1. What Is Liberal About the Liberal Arts?

It has been mentioned earlier that no course can claim any monopoly on the teaching of creativity. In the same way, no course can claim any monopoly on the "liberal" elements in the school objectives. But the question persists: Why are the liberal arts called *liberal*? In other words, what is liberal about the liberal arts?

The liberal arts — which include such areas as literature, philosophy, the fine and graphic arts, the history of thought, and music — are *supposed* to have a "liberating" effect on the mind. This liberating effect is (again *supposed* to be) brought about in two major ways:

a. The *content* of the courses is very broad in scope; it widens the students' thought horizons; and it allows the development of imagination and creativity.

b. The *methodology* employed allows for free expression in a variety of ways; it allows for a clash of ideas and for a free exchange thereof; and it is not stereo-typed, straight-jacketed, or set in its ways.

When these two elements (with their characteristics) are combined, the educational process has a stimulating as well as a liberating effect on students. The combination is essential. There are some who erroneously assume that it is the content alone that has this liberating effect automatically; it does not. A philosophy course, for example, taught by a narrow-minded person or by one who is dogmatic and inflexible, will have the exact opposite effect. It might produce radicals (equally set in the opposite viewpoints) and/or brainwashed and blind followers.

As a matter of fact and from practical experience, of the two elements (content and methodology) involved, it is the methodology that would be of a more liberating influence than the content. For even in a highly technical course, where there is very little room for personal opinion, the methodology used by the instructor may open up vistas of thought, manifestation, and application that will render the course "more liberating" (in its total effect on students) than an art course that allows students only to copy and repeat. This is precisely why, at the outset of this chapter, it was stated that the liberal arts courses are *supposed* to have a liberating effect.

More details about this liberating effect will be at least implied in the next section.

2. The Major Objectives of Teaching and Learning the Liberal Arts

A point of clarification needs to be made at this point. The major objectives of teaching various courses or academic areas are not mutually exclusive. All the objectives, or most of them, can cut across the curriculum. Whole education, as a matter of intent, would subscribe to a system where the objectives cut across the curriculum in an integrated fashion. This, however, does not preclude having a concentration of objectives in a particular area or in a set of related areas. From this point of view, the liberal arts are meant to have the following major objectives:

(Basically cognitive objectives)

a. *Students will develop their logical and analytical thinking.* By discussing a variety of social, political, economic, philosophical, scientific, and other issues, students will learn to approach these subjects methodically and analytically.

b. *Students will develop their divergent thinking.* By seeing issues from a variety of points of view, students will be encouraged to approach them through a divergent, non-authoritarian way of thinking, while retaining the possibility of injecting a convergent, authoritarian, viewpoint where the issues require it and/or when basic values are involved.

c. *Students will grow in their ability to distinguish between fact and opinion.* One of the most discouraging and disheartening occurrences is to see students (and other presumably educated persons) consistently confuse fact and opinion.

d. *Students will develop their knowledge about the world and world problems.* They will see how they and these world problems can impact upon each other.

e. *Students will come to grips with their basic beliefs and values.* By discussing major and minor issues in a variety of areas, and by interacting with these issues after a process of introspection, students will develop an understanding of where they stand in terms of their fundamental beliefs and code of values.

f. *Students will develop a clearer picture of possible vocational and avocational interests.* This is especially true when the liberal arts areas they get involved in are properly integrated with other academic areas such as mathematics, the life and physical sciences, and the social sciences.

(Basically behavioral objectives)

g. *Students will learn to articulate their thoughts precisely and succinctly both orally and in writing.* The continuous exchange of ideas and positions will help students to sharpen their use of language and make it truly communicative and effective.

h. *Students will develop skills in social dynamics.* Learning how to relate to peers and elders (teachers, parents, and other members of the community) in discourse sharpens students' social skills and dynamics and makes them more effective citizens. (See Bruell, 1991)

i. *Students will learn flexibility and adjustability.* This is not to be construed as a desire to conform, but an ability to make adjustment and accommodation, particularly to adverse positions.

j. *Students will develop their intellectual and social maturity and balance.* The intellectual challenge posed by thoughts and ideas (old and new) and the process of verbalizing positions concerning them in groups enhance social maturity, as well as personal and social balance.

k. *Students will develop their skills in service.* Taking a stand on issues, relating to others meaningfully, and having the opportunity to interact with the community can easily and surely develop the desire, the need, and the ability to be of service somewhere.

(Basically affective objectives)

l. *Students will develop their sense of tolerance.* This tolerance will apply both to the ideas and to the behavior of others.

m. *Students will develop their sense of appreciation.* This appreciation will apply to pieces of art, pieces of music, literary works, nature, discoveries, innovations, persons, cultures, beliefs, and ideas.

n. *Students will develop their sense of caring and empathy.* What is the real value of an education that is void of humane feelings?

o. *Students will develop their sensitivity.* This sensitivity will apply, among other things, to other people's needs and feelings.

p.   *Students will develop their imagination and taste.*   The enhancement of creativity and imagination is one of the greatest contributions of the liberal arts. Additionally, students will develop their own styles, which is different from just being fashionable; this is being stylish and tasteful in the fullest sense of the words.

Whole education insists on this all-rounded type of education. The development of the above objectives, while not limited to the liberal arts, must be taken seriously if we are serious about making education relevant. It is tragic enough when these objectives (especially the behavioral and affective ones) are given no more than lip service in the liberal arts courses. It is doubly tragic when courses such as art and music and drama (at least dramatic productions) are the first ones to be eliminated as a result of budget restraints and constraints. What are the students left with then? Is the total meaning of an education limited to passing test scores? When the behavioral and affective objectives are neglected (even partially), let the irrelevance of an educational system not surprise anyone. Such a system will have lost some of its finer qualities — the qualities that will ensure the nurturing of young lives to live meaningfully and be able to make a meaningful contribution as citizens and responsible and creative members of society.

3. Integrating the Liberal Arts With Other Disciplines

It is rather obvious that the objectives of teaching and learning the liberal arts are too important to neglect. Somehow these objectives, or a substantial measure thereof, need to be attained by students. As has been mentioned on more than one occasion so far, no single objective or combination of objectives is the monopoly of any course or group of courses in the curriculum. Therefore, even in the event of having to reduce the hours in, or entirely eliminate, such courses as art and music (and, in some cases, drama and physical education), it is of the essence to see to it that the major objectives mentioned above are, to some degree at least, attainable in other areas of the curriculum.

In earlier chapters, some indication was given to how certain disciplines can be integrated with other disciplines. Included in the discussion were such areas as the language arts, the social sciences, mathematics, and the life and physical sciences. To avoid redundancy, this section will not deal with the integration theme in the same manner.

Rather, an important viewpoint is presented here that should have a good number of practical advantages.

The focal point is not centered on how liberal arts content elements can be "mixed in" with other disciplines. The notion that needs to be looked at quite seriously is *how to liberalize other areas of the curriculum. The object here would be to turn the whole curriculum of the secondary school into a neatly woven, integrated whole of a liberal arts bundle with enough hands-on experience in the school and in the community to make education truly relevant to the lives of high school students.*

Let us now take this one step at a time. By truly integrating the various content elements in the curriculum with each other in a meaningful way, we would actually be helping to liberalize the curriculum. Students will not only have an academic opportunity to see the integral relationships that exist across major disciplinary areas. They will be able to find a variety of means (linguistic, artistic, musical, physical, and scientific) to express themselves freely and responsibly on any and all topics in their academic program. Injecting such an approach into the teaching of such subjects as mathematics, the life and physical sciences, and the social sciences would not only enhance the attainment of the objectives of the liberal arts; it would, additionally, help to make those very subjects more interesting and more relevant.

4. Whole Education and the Liberal Arts

Whole education views the high school curriculum essentially as a liberal education curriculum with para-vocational opportunities. This needs elaboration. The two-pronged high school curriculum should ensure

a. the attainment of the major objectives cited under the various disciplines discussed earlier and

b. the development of potential vocational or para-vocational interests and/or the nurturing of hands-on experiences in the community (primarily in the form of voluntary service) that will give students more self-esteem and make them see how relevant their academic program is to real-life situations. (More will be said about this latter point in the chapter on **Whole Education and the Community**.)

It is probably not redundant to emphasize an important point: liberalizing the curriculum (with a view to obtaining the objectives included under the teaching and learning of the liberal arts) requires much more than just liking the idea and offering lip service to it; it requires serious and rigorous planning on the basis of a fundamental change in the way the various parts of the curriculum are packaged and delivered.

Chapter Eleven

Whole Education and School Administration

1. Introduction

It is probably desirable from the outset to mention what this chapter is *not* about before going into the specific areas to be covered. There is enough written on the topics one would normally expect to find in a treatise on educational administration: organizational charts, accountability, the (traditional) role of the principal, supervising instruction, holding various types of meetings, preparing various reports, relating to the community, preparing the school budget, public relations, working on long-range plans, preparing schedules, and perhaps a few principles of educational administration as practiced in a democracy.

This is not to say that the above topics are not important. They are *very* important. This chapter, however, deals with the aspects of educational administration that are essential prerequisites for the success of a whole education approach. It is to be understood, however, that the recommendations made here are meant more as suggestions in line with a new trend or philosophy rather than as strict recipes that do not allow for any adjustment or modification.

2. The Fundamental Need and Objective: the Management of Learning

For a good number of years now there has been a trend to view educational administration (in schools, colleges, and universities) from a *management* point of view. The input in this regard from management firms and associations has been enormous. The bulk of the emphasis has focused mainly on the management of *personnel,* the management of *budgets,* the management of the *information system,* the management of *long-range plans,* and the management of other areas that are somehow *quantifiable.* Even evaluation, measurement, and the distribution of grades have been looked at managerially in quantifiable terms: curves, percentages, percentiles, averages, grade-point averages, standard deviations, and rankings. While all these matters have their place in a school administrative set-up, they do not touch (at least in any appreciable measure) upon *the most fundamental need in education and the most fundamental objective of educational administration: the effective management of learning.* Towards this end, the relevant elements pertaining to educational administration, from a whole education perspective, will be elaborated upon here. (See Bonstingl, 1992)

3. The Relevant Principles of Educational Administration
Only four such principles will be dealt with briefly.

a.   *The democratic nature of educational administration.*   It is important to live up to the principle that educational administration is democratic in its nature. But what does this actually mean in practice? It obviously could not mean the abdication of leadership in favor of "majority rule" in the school set-up. There has been some emphasis put on *participatory management* in running schools, colleges, and universities.   In a number of cases, this concept has been grossly misunderstood, misinterpreted, and misapplied. A very delicate balance is to be maintained with respect to a number of fundamental notions. The *democratic nature* of educational administration demands some form of *participatory management* on the part of faculty and staff members. *Accountability,* on the other hand, demands a much heavier *responsibility* from administrators.   The balance, therefore, between *assuming a role of responsibility* and *selling ideas* on the one hand, and *allowing for active faculty and staff participation* (commensurate with their responsibility and relative accountability) on the other, becomes very crucial.

b.   *Serving the instructional staff.* Toward greater effectiveness in the management of learning, whole education demands that the school administration (through the principal, an assistant principal, or a professional educator designated by the principal) go much beyond serving the instructional staff simply by providing the usual facilities (offices, equipment, books, aids, etc.) and demanding the usual requirements (unit and lesson plans, attendance sheets, grade books, meetings, parental contacts, reporting etc.). The service called for here is to include *leading, guiding, supervising, training, retraining,* and *retooling* teachers to become progressively more effective in the whole education process and techniques.

c. *Axing and X-ing the Peter Principle.* Why is it that in practically every educational set-up (school, board, district, county, etc.) there is a blatant application of the Peter Principle (Peter and Hull, 1969)? Very often this is the one major cause of failure, mediocrity, unhappiness, unfairness, and demoralization. Whole education insists on having students capitalize on their talents, interests, and strengths in learning new subjects and going through new experiences; students will find their course work and schooling more relevant when they are allowed to pursue areas that are of greatest interest to them and involve themselves in endeavors that help actualize their potential. Whole education hopes that the same principle and practice will apply to teachers, staff members, and administrators in such a way that no person will be allowed to function in any capacity at a level of incompetence and inefficiency. Let every person do what she/he can do best and most effectively. At the expense of stifling meaningless "promotions", this will ensure a greater measure of fairness, happiness, and productivity in both the short and the long runs.

d. *Public Relations and the Community.* A considerable portion of administrative time should rightfully and justifiably be spent on the promotion of public relations and the development of effective liaisoning with the community. It is not only the moral and financial support of the community that is required. It is much more than that. Of vital importance to the success of whole education is the active, positive, and productive participation of the community and its various sectors in the promotion of relevant field experiences for students. (A more detailed presentation of these field experiences is found in Chapter Twelve.)

4. The General School Climate as Seen by Visitors

What a difference the school atmosphere or general climate can make! Just as visitors enter a school building, they can sense the warmth and congeniality in the atmosphere. It is to some extent, of course, a sixth sense that makes some visitors feel that. But there are several other small and big signs and manifestations that contribute to the general wholesomeness of a school climate; and it is usually the small manifestations that strike visitors for a first, and often lasting, impression. For the purpose of making concerned personnel conscious of such elements, a few positive ones are given here:

- clean grounds and neatly marked parking areas,
- spotless hallways,
- neat and clear signs leading to the main office,
- pictures, sayings, bulletin boards, and murals artistically displayed in the hallways,
- the neatness and orderly behavior of persons (particularly students and teachers) walking in the hallways,
- the neatness and general look of the main office,
- the warm welcome (and smiles) given by the office staff,
- the efficiency and effectiveness of the school staff in answering questions, meeting needs, and dispatching business,
- the presence in school of parents and other members of the community to ask questions, make requests, and/or volunteer services, and
- the availability of yearbooks, brochures, catalogs, and other school publications that serve as public relations instruments.

Visitors also have a chance to witness and sense the school climate by attending a variety of school functions such as exhibits, dramatic productions, open houses, social parties, P.T.A. meetings, commencement exercises, and the like.

All of these and other manifestations would give some indication to visitors about the tempo, the friendliness, the warmth, the standards, the effectiveness and efficiency, and the general atmosphere in a school.

The following section also deals, to some extent, with the general climate of a school as brought about through the relations of the principal and other administrative staff members with other persons in the school and the community.

5. The Principal's Relations

On my first visit to a particular high school to observe one of my student teachers, I was shocked at what I saw: dirty hallways, untidy classes, rather unruly behavior by most students, tardy students walking into the classroom nonchalantly, and so on. After my observation, upon remarking about the state of affairs, I got this reply from the cooperating teacher: "The principal doesn't care." The first requirement for a school atmosphere that is conducive to effective teaching, effective learning, and desirable personal and social behavior is a *caring principal*. Obviously, that alone will not do it, but it is the first requirement.

Next in importance as essential requirements are the relations that the principal holds with teachers, staff members, students, and parents.

a. *Relations with teachers and staff members*. Whatever the school philosophy is and whatever the objectives are, the key to the success of the educational operation is the wholesome personal and professional relations that the principal (as chief educational executive officer) holds with teachers and members of the staff. Just as students need to be motivated, encouraged, guided, assisted, praised, and, when the occasion demands it, reminded of their shortcomings, so teachers and members of the staff expect to receive the same from the principal. It is a responsibility that should never be shirked.

This, of course, is nothing new, but whole education makes special demands of the principal in this respect to ensure the success and effectiveness of the educative process. Beyond the commonly accepted norms governing the relations of the principal with teachers and staff members, whole education would insist on the following attitudes and procedures:

(with teachers)

• Be positive (and encouraging) at all times.

• Guide the integrative planning of the curriculum. (See Cornbleth, 1990)

• Insist on the importance and practice of teacher role models. (Whatever teachers demand in the way of behavior, they should practice; and whatever they prohibit, they must refrain from doing themselves.)

• Help plan exchange class visitations.

• Support the teachers in every way (morally and otherwise).

• Give innovative suggestions to make whole education work, and make allowances for imperfections.

• Insist on proper grooming and dress (appropriate, not over-done) that will help spell the climate and provide a good impression.

• Insist on standards of appropriate personal and professional behavior by teachers in school and in the community.

• In general, set the standard high and expect matching

performance.
- Make the teachers proud of their school.

(with staff members)
- Insist on efficiency (punctuality, knowledge about particular responsibilities, general knowledge about the school, and handling issues with dispatch).
- Insist on proper grooming and dress (appropriate, not over-done) that will help spell the climate and provide a good impression.
- Insist on standards of appropriate personal and professional behavior by staff members in school and in the community.
- Insist on the avoidance of behavior that builds negative impressions: over-chatting, chewing gum on the job, eating in offices, etc.
- Insist on the important element of courtesy on the part of all staff members with anyone they deal with.
- Insist on a team spirit that will make cooperation and pitching in for others a matter of habit.
- Be supportive in every way (morally and otherwise).
- Solicit their opinion. (Very often they are the most knowledgeable in certain situations.)
- In general, set the standard high and expect matching performance.
- Make all the staff members (from vice-principals to custodial staff) proud of their school.

b. *Relations with students.* The tempo, the tone, the spirit, the overall climate in a school are, to a great extent, brought about and influenced by the relations that the principal has with students. Too many principals, unfortunately, insulate themselves from other persons in the school, especially students, the assumption being that other people in the school (namely, teachers and counselors) are entrusted with student affairs. This is not only unfortunate; it can be treacherous. The more successful schools are the ones that witness a direct relationship between the chief executives (principal and vice-principals) and the students. It is not uncommon for some principals to know the students by name — especially the ones in the upper classes.

Two important matters that have already been mentioned demand a direct relationship, at some time or another, between the principal and the students: the administration of whole education is primarily concerned with the *management of learning,* and the first requirement of a successful administration is a *caring principal.*

Students meet challenges and live up to expectations. When they see that the principal *cares* about them and *expects* a particular standard of behavior (academically, personally, and socially), they will (especially if other essential ingredients are also present) live up to those expectations. Very often, unfortunately, students' abilities, potential, and capacities are underestimated. Students — all students — the highly talented, the average, the slow learning, and the learning-disabled — have enormous abilities and capacities that need to be discovered, encouraged, nurtured, and allowed to be fulfilled. A principal's personal interest in their welfare, manifested in both occasional and sustained relations, will go a long way towards bringing about a conducive atmosphere for learning and towards achieving pupil purposes and objectives. With this in mind, it would behoove principals to take heed of the following points:

- Make yourself available (certain hours a week) to students.
- Occasionally walk the corridors and stop and chat with students.
- Send congratulatory memos when achievements warrant the gesture.
- Take an interest in their work: displays, exhibits, murals, essays, publications, competitions, etc.
- Attend as many student functions as you can: sports meets, dramatic productions, oratorical contests, debates, etc.
- Insist on standards of appropriate personal and social behavior.
- Be an example and torch bearer of the standards you preach and teach.
- Make certain that the students receive their full rights and that they respond with a commensurate measure of responsibility.
- Show an interest in the students' lives and conditions.
- Do everything possible (especially with the students) to make all students proud of their school while they are in it and supportive of it in the future.

c.   *Relations with parents.*   What could constitute a better combination than a caring principal, caring teachers, and caring parents? And if the parents happen not to care or not have the time to exhibit care, then the principal and teachers can make up for that, on the one hand, and try to make the parents more involved, on the other. The following points may be helpful to administrators:

• Keep in touch with parents or guardians on all matters related to the life and academic work of students.

• Try to involve the parents as much as possible in school affairs and activities.

• Keep the parents informed about the school: objectives, curriculum, activities, needs, etc.

• Solicit the help of parents in school affairs and activities.

• Solicit the help of able parents in whole education activities.

• Solicit the support of parents in every way: financially, professionally, at board meetings, etc.

• Make the parents proud of their children and their school.

Chapter Twelve

Whole Education and the Community

1. Introduction

The school is one of the institutions of society. The more successful schools — i.e., the schools that ultimately give their students a better rounded and a more wholesome education — are the ones that have managed to become an integral part of their community and society. Unfortunately, in the vast majority of cases, the schools are *isolated* from their communities and *insulated* from them. This factor alone can, over a period of time, erode the relevance of an educational program. When additionally, the program itself has little bearing on what is going on in the larger community, the irrelevance can grow to enormous and dangerous proportions.

What are the symptoms or manifestations of a school-society relationship that make the school an integral part of the society or community it serves? There are several. Some of the more common ones are the following:

- moral (and in some cases, financial) support of the school by the community,
- an active P. T. A. (Parent-Teacher Association),
- volunteer work (typing, substitute teaching, directing extra-class activities, etc.) by parents and other members of the community,
- community visits to the school for a variety of activities: sports, exhibits, displays, dramatic productions, open houses, convocations, assemblies, lectures, concerts, commencement exercises, and the like,
- involvement of the school administrators, faculty, and staff in community activities and civic duties,
- friendly and wholesome relations between school personnel

(and students) and different members and agencies of the community: shops and shopping malls, hospitals, the police, the fire department, the public library, churches, clubs, recreational facilities, and so on,

• decent and orderly behavior of students in the community, and

• a responsible board of education with support from the community.

It is very obvious that the community is an immense resource — with practically unlimited possibilities — that can be easily tapped for greater educational effectiveness both quantitatively and qualitatively. This greater effectiveness will benefit the students, of course, but it can also be designed to benefit other members of the community as well. Towards this end, a number of venues will be examined as examples of what can be done to provide the students with a more effective educational program that will help fill the relevance gap and at the same time make the students develop their self-concept and self-worth. (See Taylor, Vlastos, and Wise, 1989-92)

2. Work in the Community for Credit

With cooperation from various sectors and agencies in the community, it is envisaged for each student in the eleventh and twelfth grades to give one hundred hours (more for extra credit) a year in community service. This would be for academic credit, which could be lumped totally under *community service* or partially (say 50%) under *community service* and partially (50% in one area or 25% in each of two areas) under other subject areas, depending on where the work was done, what area it fitted under, and the level and quality of the work performed. Extra credit (for at least 25 hours a year and no more than 50 hours a year) can be similarly applied. (See Schlechty, 1992)

Following are some suggestions (by no means exhaustive) that could provide very desirable experiences for students:

a. *Work in hospitals and first aid stations.* This kind of work will develop the students' knowledge of anatomy, physiology, and/or health care. (Possible credit in the sciences.)

b. *Work in nursing homes and hospices.* This will not only develop the students' knowledge and skills in handling senior citizens in need, but it will also nurture the students' affective sense of caring. (Possible credit in the sciences.)

c. *Work with the fire department and/or emergency units.* This can involve anything from driving ambulances and cars to administering resuscitation procedures and first aid techniques. (Possible credit in the sciences and/or social science.)

d. *Work with illiterates.* If a community happens to have native illiterates, much work will be needed to rectify the situation. Literacy programs can be very fascinating and challenging. (Possible credit in English or social science.)

e. *ESL classes and orientation programs for new immigrants.* If a community happens to have newly arrived immigrants, work will be needed to teach them English and to orient them to American culture and to the American way of life. (Possible credit in English and/or social science.)

f. *Providing a mentor program.* Junior and senior high school students are in an excellent position to provide private lessons and tutorials for elementary or junior high students in the subjects which they are good at. This near-peer teaching can provide much needed help to the tutees and a very enriching experience to the tutors. (Possible credit in social science or any of the subjects taught.)

g. *Work in police stations.* This can take the form of clerical and office work at the station or minor ride-along duties, especially if some of the minor offenses are committed by young teenagers. (Possible credit in social science.)

h. *Work in courts of law.* This can involve note-taking, typing procedures, or assisting lawyers, prosecutors, and judges. (Possible credit in social science.)

i. *Providing home-work hot lines.* This would be a service to students below eleventh grade level who need particular (unscheduled) help with homework. (Possible credit in relevant subjects.)   (See Solomon and Scott, 1988 and Singh, 1987)

j. *Work in industrial complexes.* This will orient students to the various types of industries, the scientific angles of the work, the financial aspects involved, and the human relations side of running the industries. The work performed can take any number of forms, depending on need and on the particular talents and interests of students. (Possible credit in relevant subjects.)

k. *Work in banks and financial institutions.* Here mathematics can come alive, and if the students can work at something requiring calculations, the benefit would be immeasurable. (Possible credit in mathematics.)

l. *Work with the physically and/or learning-disabled.* Apart from the knowledge and skills learned that are related to the needs of physically and learning-disabled persons, there is much to say about the development of the affective sense of caring. (Possible credit in relevant subjects.)

m. *Providing Saturday morning fillers for youngsters in the community.* This would involve working with children of different age groups, conducting such activities as story-telling, game-playing, volunteer work in specific parts of the community, or any other wholesome activity. (Possible credit in social science.)

n. *Work in child care centers.* This can be a meaningful experience for students who like children and/or students who might be interested in a major in child development. The work can take a variety of forms. (Possible credit in social science.)

o. *Individualized, home-centered child care work.* This would be child care per se or instruction in child care to parents who need it in the community. (Possible credit in social science.)

p. *Work with engineers, architects, and/or designers.* This is where geometry and art can come alive. This work can be very creative and challenging. (Possible credit in mathematics and/or art.)

q. *Work in community projects.* This would involve students in any of the projects sponsored by the community or any sector of it. It could involve work on construction sites, in the public library, in clean-up campaigns, in poster-making, in delivering "Meals on Wheels", or any project that requires volunteers. (Possible credit in relevant subjects.)

r. *Work in hotels, restaurants, or business enterprises.* If meaningful work can be planned for students in any of these spheres, it would be worthwhile for them to experience the functioning of a small business in practice. (Possible credit in relevant subjects.)

s. *Work in school.* This could be a matter of assisting an administrator, a librarian, or a teacher. The work, of course, would have to be challenging, a learning experience, and a rewarding experience. (Possible credit in relevant subjects.)

t. *Work in recreational centers.* This can take the form of social work and interpersonal relations in games or discussions, or it can take the form of some physical exercises and training. It would be particularly helpful to youngsters in these recreational centers. (Possible credit in health, physical education, social science, and/or the sciences.)

For this to work out optimally and effectively, a concerted effort is needed on the part of the school (administrators, teachers, and students), the parents, and the community at large (civic leaders, businessmen, organizations, professionals, social workers, and all those engaged in different projects and enterprises).

With the community coming into the school for various functions and volunteer work, and with the school reaching out into the community by having high school volunteers do meaningful work in the community, there will truly be an active school-community integration and interaction to the benefit of all. Developing a micro-society in school, as has been practiced in certain areas, may be a very small step in the right direction, but it falls way short of what can be accomplished through whole education.

3. Benefits from Work in the Community

Some of the benefits emanating from work in the community may be very obvious, while others may not be so obvious. Whole education not only supports the concept of student work in the community, but requires it for the following major advantages:

a. Work in the community boosts a student's self-concept, self-image, and self-worth; it also gives the student a sense of being needed.

b. Academic performance in practically all subjects will improve, in some cases even dramatically.

c. Exposure to different types of work ("employment") can be a source of some income, although the basic emphasis should be on *volunteer work*.

d. The exposure may lead to full-time employment for school leavers.

e. The exposure may motivate students to major in the field that they did work in and enjoyed.

f. Students will definitely have less time (and basically a diminishing desire) for loitering, TV watching, smoking, drinking, drug using, and other undesirables.

g. The quality of interaction among school friends, home members, and in the community will be boosted, since hundreds of students will be doing something worthwhile and expressing themselves about it and exchanging views on it.

h. Wherever the work is done (homes, schools, offices, agencies, etc.), the recipients of the student services will have their lots, situations, standards, and work improved.

i. There will be a general improvement in the atmosphere of the community, since so many students will be contributing in various ways to its well-being.

j. Parents will be very happy with, and proud of, their schools and their children.

k. Students will sharpen their sense of responsibility by actually assuming responsibilities in a variety of spheres.

l. Students will learn the value of time. They will learn to be punctual, and they will develop skills in budgeting their own time, a necessary skill in life.

m. Every student will have a place in school and in the community. This, in a very real way, will compensate for the fact that in many classes and schools, the average (balanced, well-behaved) students tend to be neglected.

n. The community at large will feel excited about the schools and develop a sense of caring about the students (as persons and citizens), especially as the students will be making such a needed and meaningful contribution to the life of the community.

The schools should be prepared to give students a new lease on life. By coordinating their work with various sectors of the community, and by having the community provide cognate experiences for the students, the schools will be doing just that.

Chapter Thirteen

The Implementation of Whole Education

1. Introduction

The presentation so far has hopefully made it amply clear that *whole education* represents a new trend in handling the entire educational operation as it applies to the secondary school. It would be erroneous to assume that dealing with one or two or even a few of the angles and facets referred to would solve the problems faced in secondary education today. No patchwork solution is going to provide an adequate answer to the serious problems facing secondary education. To eradicate or wipe out the *relevance gap* in existence now — or, at least, to lessen its impact appreciably — all fronts on the education scene should be faced head-on.

As has been mentioned earlier, *whole education* does not subscribe to any one particular formula. The sky's the limit for original approaches and creative innovations in content and methodology. This, of course, is in reference to the curricular content prescribed and the educational methods used by schools and teachers. The same principle holds true for the recommendations suggested in this chapter. They are not meant to represent a fixed formula for implementing the principles and practices of *whole education*. They are meant as suggestions representing a new trend in secondary education. But, while the specific suggestions and recommendations may be modified in ways to suit particular situations and conditions, it is important to realize that *all* the areas mentioned should be tackled together, in whatever fashion, to bring about the desired changes and results. (See Toch, 1991)

2. The Major Objectives of Whole Education

To have a clear idea about these desired changes and results, the major objectives of *whole education* are presented here in two parts: the positive and the negative. It is good to know what we want to accomplish (the positive ends) and what we want to avoid or reduce or even eliminate (the negative ends).

a.   *The positive objectives.* Briefly stated, the major positive objectives of *whole education* are the following:

- to enhance the student's self-image,
- to enhance the student's worth to others,
- to motivate students to work harder on school subjects,
- to motivate students to find their proper places in society as responsible members and citizens,
- to make education relevant to the lives of students,
- to raise academic standards in all subjects,
- to develop wholesome vocational and avocational interests,
- to attain international competitiveness in all areas, and
- to create a healthier and more wholesome climate at home, in school, and in the community.

b.   *The negative objectives.* Briefly stated, the major negative objectives of *whole education* are the following:

- to reduce or eliminate the boredom, disinterest, and despondency felt by students,
- to reduce or eliminate the attrition and drop-out rates in school,
- to reduce or eliminate the relevance gap in education,
- to reduce or eliminate idleness and the meaningless use of time,
- to reduce or eliminate the use of alcohol and drugs, and
- to reduce or eliminate undesirable behavior, including the commitment of crimes and other unlawful acts.

3. Practical Recommendations

Towards fulfilling the (positive and negative) objectives mentioned above, the following practical recommendations are made. These recommendations are not necessarily summaries of points made earlier. For more details connected with the recommendations, it may be good to review the relevant sections in the book.

a.   *Recommendations pertaining to the curriculum.* At the heart of the *whole education* approach is an over-hauled curriculum. This is precisely where the *directional change* and the *qualitative change* alluded to earlier reside.

• *Extend the school day* by one hour to 3:00 p.m. (For eleventh and twelfth graders, four school days can be extended to 4:00 p.m., thus allowing one morning and one afternoon a week, in addition to Saturdays, for community work.)

• *Extend the school year* to at least 210 school days.

• *Restate the general school objectives* and the objectives of the various disciplinary areas or integrated groups of disciplines. Examine these objectives periodically and make certain that everybody concerned (teachers, students, and parents or guardians) has these objectives constantly in mind.

• *Make certain that all the activities* (class activities as well as out-of-class activities) sponsored by the school *are designed and prescribed as vehicles for the attainment of the stated objectives.*

• *Make certain that the various teaching aids and methodologies employed are similarly geared to achieve the objectives.*

• *Integrate different disciplinary areas* in a meaningful and practical fashion to enhance the relevance of the subjects to the students. (Examples: All disciplines can permeate certain elements of the language arts classes at least in terms of reading material to be handled like any piece of literature. Language standards and requirements can be applied in all other disciplines. The sciences and the social sciences can be made to relate to each other, at least in certain areas, very effectively. The arts can permeate all other disciplines.)

• *Design particular science sequences in an integrative manner* to make them interesting, relevant, practical, and rigorous at the same time. If such sequences are designed effectively, there will be no reason why students would not want to delve into the sciences and, as a result, have the equivalent (overall) of a whole year of each of biology, chemistry, physics, and earth science over a four-year period. (Schools in many parts of the world require such equivalents.)

• *Design a new Mathematics for Life course* and require it of all students. (See Chapter Nine for more details.)

• *Design another General Mathematics course* to include elements of algebra, plane geometry, and a dash of design and solid geometry in a practical, down-to-earth manner. (If the Mathematics for Life course is a success, students would want to take the General Mathematics course as an elective if it is not required.)

• *Try to liberalize all courses,* especially in the non-restrictive methodology used.

• *Integrate the curriculum with community life* in such a way that ninth and tenth graders have a real first-hand look at what is going on in various fields of endeavor in the community as observers and in such a way that eleventh and twelfth graders have a real hands-on experience working in the community as volunteers.

• *Prepare integrative materials* for the various courses and sequences of courses until such time as more appropriate textbooks are available as added choices.

(For more details regarding different aspects of the curriculum, refer to Chapters Five through Ten.)

b. *Recommendations pertaining to students.* The focal point of interest in the *whole education* approach is the *individual learner.* The directional and qualitative changes envisaged are meant to serve the individual learner much more effectively.

• *Get the students enthused* about the new program. When they know that their lives will be touched by the new approach and that they will be active participants in it, they will be highly *motivated* to become a part of it.

• *Prepare a data sheet* for each student to include information regarding background, interests, hobbies, special talents, strengths, weaknesses, etc.

• *Use the data sheet to analyze the student's needs and best channels of activity.*

• *Design a tentative individualized four-year program* for each student to include the academic courses of study and possible areas of observation and work in the community.

• *Update the individualized program periodically,* making desirable adjustments according to changing needs and interests.

• *Provide different channels for students to express themselves* in school and in the community about their program of study and community activities.

(For more details regarding students as individual learners, refer to Chapter Three.)

c. *Recommendations pertaining to teachers.* The teachers represent the front line in dealing with and handling students. Everything possible should be done to encourage teachers to move in the direction of *whole education,* and every provision should be made to facilitate their task.

• *Get the teachers enthused* about the new whole education program.

• *Encourage the teachers* to know more about whole education (its objectives, philosophy of approach, and innovative methodology) and to discuss whole education professionally with their colleagues.

• *Help train, retrain, and retool teachers* to become progressively more effective as whole education teachers.

• *Assign different tasks to different teachers* in accordance with their talents and interests. Not all teachers need to do the same thing in the same way. Whole education is designed to be flexible and to make the best use of every teacher's special skills and abilities.

• *Reduce the teachers' teaching contact hours* proportionately to allow more planning and coordinating time for some of them.

• *Encourage the professional growth of teachers,* especially in areas that would make them more effective whole education teachers.

(For more details regarding different aspects of teachers' work as learning facilitators, refer to Chapter Four.)

d. *Recommendations pertaining to school administrators.* The school administrators are the primary facilitators of teachers' work. The tone that they set in school and in the community, as well as the care that they exhibit for the teachers' and students' welfare, would go a long way towards making education a much more successful venture.

• *Create a positive and wholesome climate in school.* Care for teachers' and students' welfare.

• *Be efficient in dealing with people.* Handle all requests and problems courteously and with dispatch.

• *Help teachers in their planning of whole education programs.* It is important for teachers to know that you are behind them and their efforts.

• *Make yourselves available to students.* This will greatly help in creating rapport and cooperation.

• *Set the standards high for teachers and students.* The behavioral response will hopefully always match the expectations.

• *Relate well to parents and guardians.* They are the ones most concerned about their children's welfare.

• *Relate well to community leaders and the public in general.* Community support (moral, financial, and professional) is vital for the success of any school.

- *Solicit the cooperation of parents and community leaders in the school program.*
- *Solicit funds from foundations and/or the community* to finance different aspects of the whole education program.
- (For state departments of education) *Think of, plan, and devise alternative certification requirements.* The school systems are the losers for missing the services of highly talented and richly experienced persons who might not meet the straight-jacketed certification requirements, but who are otherwise extremely capable of teaching and providing high caliber role models.
- (For schools of education)   Beyond meeting state certification requirements, *be innovative and flexible in providing more choices, electives, and alternative routes in degree programs.*

(For more details regarding school administration, refer to Chapter Eleven.)

e. *Recommendations pertaining to parents and guardians.*   The parents and guardians are the ones most concerned about their children's welfare.   Additionally, the school needs their support.

- *Take an interest in what the school is doing.* Keep abreast of the information given out by the school, and constantly ask your sons and daughters about their activities.
- *Attend as many school functions as possible.* These include exhibits, displays, open houses, dramatic productions, debates, lecture series, P.T.A. meetings, sports meets, socials, commencement exercises, and the like.
- *Volunteer your services to the school* in ways that you are competent in and comfortable with.
- *Support the school morally and otherwise.* The school serves your children. It behooves you to offer as much help to the school as you possibly can.
- *Promote the welfare of the school in the community.*

f. *Recommendations pertaining to the community.*   The school is an integral part of the community.   All members of the community should exhibit a real interest in what goes on in the school. The teenagers in the community represent a formidable portion of, and force in, the community. Showing a vital interest in the school and providing it with the needed help and support might spell the difference between a problem-ridden community and a happy, peaceful, and relatively problem-free community.

- *Take an interest in what the school is doing.*
- *Attend as many school functions as possible.*
- *Volunteer your services to the school.* This may take the form of service performed in school (typing, lecturing, conducting some extra-class activities, and the like) or it may take the form of opening your place of work or business to students for observation or volunteer service.
- *Support the school morally and financially.*
- *Promote the welfare of the school in the community* to such an extent that the school can be a source of pride for you in the community and a positive landmark for you to show visitors to your area.
- *Promote your own business by providing funds* to the school to finance projects or innovative experiments.
- *Help to make all the institutions of your community act as a cohesive whole.* Your community, as a result, will be a much happier place to live in.

(For more details regarding community participation and student work in the community, refer to Chapter Twelve.)

Chapter Fourteen

Conclusion

1. Revolution Or Evolution?

If it is quality education that we are seeking, there is no escape from whole education. It may be thought by some that whole education is essentially a natural outcome of our past experiences in the field of teaching and learning — i.e., an outcome of our past successes and failures in the field on a world-wide basis. Some educators, on the other hand, may misinterpret whole education as representing a revolutionary trend.

To think of whole education as revolutionary is to misinterpret whole education and to misunderstand the process of education in principle. Nothing effective can be brought about in the educative process in a revolutionary manner. The process of education is essentially evolutionary in nature. To bring about effective outcomes in any educational endeavor or venture, three types of effort are required:

    a. a purposeful effort,

    b. a sustained effort, and

    c. a concerted effort.

A *purposeful effort* is most essential because clear aims and objectives are a key to success. As a matter of fact, success itself is measured against the original set of aims and objectives. It must be admitted, though, that having objectives does not, in and of itself, guarantee success or any measure of it. But to have clear and attainable objectives and to exert an effort towards achieving those objectives can make all the difference in the world in at least two ways: the objectives themselves provide a reliable yardstick by which to measure success, failure, or any change in outcomes; they also provide justification for any sense of accomplishment ensuing from the effort.

A *sustained effort* is required to maintain continuity and consistency. Well begun may be half done, but for a complete job to be done, there must be a continuous, uninterrupted, endeavor and effort to see the venture through. A sustained effort also means that all the related and relevant factors at work around the intended purpose are made to contribute to the effort and that all unrelated and irrelevant factors are not allowed to interfere in the process or affect the outcome.

A *concerted effort* is required because all the persons who are related to, or concerned with, either the activity or the major role players in the activity must become involved in one way or another (by participating, helping, encouraging, promoting, counseling, advising, sharing, caring, etc.) to make some contribution towards the success of the operation.

To think of whole education, on the other hand, as a natural outcome of our total past experiences in education does not necessarily represent the whole truth about it. Natural outcomes of any experience may be construed to depict further action in the same vein or direction as past experience. While whole education is not meant even as a revolutionary *idea*, it does imply a basic change in direction and orientation. To view each particular area, field, or discipline as a separate compartment or department is to have a *linear view* of education. A linear view compartmentalizes knowledge and makes education rigid, confined, and irrelevant. An interdisciplinary approach to education, relating a variety of subject areas to each other, spells a marked improvement, but it does not go far enough, because it is only *two-dimensional.* Whole education is *three-dimensional.* It does not only relate subjects to each other in a much broader and deeper fashion than in an interdisciplinary curriculum, but it proceeds to relate these disciplines and areas of knowledge and skill to each student's life experience in her/his community and environment, making the process of education an integral part of a student's total life and experience. Whole education relates knowledge, skills, attitudes, and feelings by making the process of education a meaningful and relevant experience to each individual student.

There is no fixed formula for whole education. The first step to be taken is a profound commitment to this approach. Beyond this commitment, the sky's the limit in terms of form and innovation.

Schools of education need to train their prospective teachers in a way that will make them not only receptive to the concept of whole education, but also to equip them with the knowledge, skills, and experience to contribute to the whole education process in an innovative way. Teachers in service need to be oriented to the new approach in seminars, workshops and both summer and evening courses. Textbooks need to be rewritten to cut across disciplines and provide students with lively, wholesome, and meaningful experiences. Parents and members of the community need to be informed about this approach and given ample means of making vital contributions to it by actively participating in the process in all kinds of ways. (See Agresto, 1991)

Students involved in whole education should bubble with enthusiasm not only because what they are learning is interesting and relevant, but also because, through the process, they are made to be active participants in real-life activities and experiences. This should have a two-fold benefit for students: individually by making them realize what roles they can play with each other and in society and, even more importantly, by making them discover who they really are.

2. A Word of Caution

It is usually not advisable to end a treatise on a negative note. The three points raised here, though, are unavoidable, and they should be taken more for their positive implications than for their negative insinuations.

a. The first of these cautionary points has to do with the limitations of whole education when applied to students with learning disabilities. Whole education may at first present some hurdles when applied with students suffering from dyslexia, autism, aphasia, mental retardation, cerebral palsy, and Downe Syndrome. A more individualized approach is recommended in cases where disabilities exist. Whenever any aspect of whole education, however, can be used successfully and comfortably, it can be tried to the extent that it works; and when it does work, the results and achievements can reach proportions beyond anyone's expectation. This in itself can be the most meaningful answer to those students' needs.

b. The second point concerns students who may need remediation in one or more areas. In such cases, remedial work, by definition, will have to be concentrated on the areas where weaknesses exist. Especially is this true where the remediation is in the sphere of skills rather than knowledge. With skills, practice makes permanent (not perfect), and practice is usually concentrated on one skill at a time.

c. The last cautionary point relates to normal students with varying abilities whose styles of learning are such that they respond more positively to the parts than to the whole. A whole education approach, thrust upon them too soon, may have adverse educational consequences. A holistic approach, for such students, may be introduced gradually when they are truly ready for it. It is only then that they will respond to it positively, enthusiastically, and successfully.

Notes and Selected References

Agresto, John, "The Failure of American Education as Both a Radical and a Conservative Enterprise", in Stephen M. Krason (Editor), *The Recovery of American Education: Reclaiming a Vision*, University Press of America, Lanham, MD 1991, pp. 1-8.

America 2000: an Education Strategy: Sourcebook, U.S. Government Printing Office, 1991, pp. 59-65.

Barnes, Douglas, *From Communication to Curriculum* (Second Edition), Boyton/Cook Publishers, Heineman, Portsmouth, NH. 1992, pp. 139-157.

Blaisdell, Muriel L., "Academic Integration: Going Beyond Disciplinary Boundaries," in Laurie Richlin (Editor), *Preparing Faculty for the New Conceptions of Scholarship*, Jossey-Bass Publishers, San Francisco, 1993, pp. 57-68.

Bonstingl, John Jay, *Schools of Quality: an Introduction to Total Quality Management in Education*, Association for Supervision and Curriculum Development, Alexandria, VA, 1992, pp. 6-19.

Bruell, Christopher, "Liberal Education and Education for Citizenship", in Stephen M. Krason (Editor), *The Recovery of American Education: Reclaiming a Vision*, University Press of America, Lanham, MD, 1991, pp. 75-86.

The Condition of Education 1992, National Center for Education Statistics, U.S. Department of Education, 1992, pp. 42-50 and 27.

Cornbleth, Catherine, *Curriculum in Context*, The Falmer Press, Bristol, PA, 1990, pp. 155-168 and 174-179.

Deal, Terence E., "School Culture: Balancing Tradition and Innovation", *Independent Schools Independent Thinkers*, edited by Pearl Rock Kane, Jossey-Base Publishers, San Francisco, CA 1992, pp. 234-245.

Digest of Education Statistics 1992, National Center for Education Statistics, U.S. Department of Education, 1992, pp. 181 and 142.

Elam, Stanley M., Lowell C. Rose, and Alec M. Gallup, "The Annual Gallup Poll of the Public's Attitudes Toward the Public Schools", *Phi Delta Kappan*, September 1991, pp. 41-56.

Gillis, Candida, *The Community as Classroom: Integrating School and Community Through Language Arts*, Heinemann, Portsmouth, NH, 1991.

Keen, John, *Language and the English Curriculum*, Open University Press, Buckingham, England, 1992, p. 40.

Marsh, Colin J., *Key Concepts for Understanding Curriculum*, The Falmer Press, Birston, PA, 1992, pp. 51-57.

The National Council on Education Standards and Testing, *Raising Standards for American Education: a Report to Congress, the Secretary of Education, the National Education Goals Panel, and the American People*, Washington, DC, January 24, 1992, pp. 9 and 27.

Page, Reba and Linda Valli, "Curriculum Differentiation: an Introduction" and "Differentiation: A Conclusion", in *Curriculum Differentiation: Interpretive Studies in U.S. Secondary Schools*, edited by Reba Page and Linda Valli, State University of New York Press, Albany, NY, 1990, pp. 1-15 and 231-242.

Peter, Laurence F., and Raymond Hull, *The Peter Principle*, William Morrow and Company, Inc., New York, 1969, p. 16.

Schlecty, P.C., *Schools for the 21st Century*, Jossey-Bass Publishers, San Francisco, CA, 1992.

Schubert, William H., "Curriculum Reform", *Challenges and Achievements of American Education: the 1993 ASCD Yearbook*, edited by Gordon Cawelti, Association for Supervision and Curriculum Development, Alexandria, VA, 1993, pp. 80-111.

Short, Kathy G. and Carolyn Burke, *Creating Curriculum; Teachers and Students as a Community of Learners*, Heinemann Educational Books, Inc., Portsmouth, NH, 1991, pp. 9-32.

Sigel, Roberta S., "Democracy in the Multi-Ethnic Society", and Marilyn Hoskin, "The Challenge of the Multi-Ethnic Society", in Roberta S. Siegel and Marilyn Hoskin (Editors), *Education for Democratic Citizenship: Challenge for Multi-Ethnic Societies*, Laurence Erlbaum Associates, Publishers, Hillsdale, NJ, 1991, pp. 3-19.

Singh, Balwaut, "Homework and Homework Hotlines: Views of Junior High School Students, Teachers, and Parents", *Spectrum*, Volume 5, No. 3, Summer, 1987, pp. 14-18.

Solomon, Alan and Leotine Scott, "Project HELP - the Home Education Learning Project: A History and Analysis of a Telephone Assistance Program for Homework", a paper presented at the Annual Meeting of the American Educational Research Association (New Orleans, LA, April 5-9) 1988.

Staszewski, James J., *Skill and Skilled Memory. Final Report. Research Report.* Office of Naval Research, Arlington, VA. Cognitive and Neural Sciences Division, 1990.

Taylor, A. and G. Vlastos, B. Wise, and J. Wise, *Head Start Classroom of the Future*, Preliminary Reports to Health and Human Services, Albuquerque, NM: University of New Mexico, 1989-92.

Toch, Thomas, *In the Name of Excellence: the Struggle to Reform the Nation's Schools, Why It's Failing, and What Should Be Done*, Oxford University Press, New York, 1991, pp. 40-71.

Yager, R.E., ed. *What Research Says to the Science Teacher:* Volume F. Washington, DC: National Science Teachers Association, 1993.

Index

A

abundant living 5
administration 89, 90, 108
affective 26, 28, 29, 65, 69, 85, 86, 98, 100
Afro-Americans 59
Agresto, John 113, 115
algebra 73, 74
Amendments 59
American, Native 59
anatomy 63
animate 63, 65
anthropology, physical 63
aphasia 113
architects 100
arithmetic 74
art 9, 76, 86
arts 2, 67, 105
astronomy 63, 75
astro-physics 63
atmosphere 7, 91, 102
attitude 11, 23, 24, 30, 48, 58, 60, 65, 112

aural 46
autism 113
avocational 68, 85, 104
axioms 74

B

banks 99
behavior 15, 27, 30, 39, 40, 55, 56, 58, 67, 85, 92, 93, 95, 104
behavioral 26, 29, 48, 56, 85, 86, 108
biochemistry 63
biology 9, 63, 75, 105
Bonstingl, John J. 90, 115
bookkeeping 74
botany 63
Bruell, Christopher 85, 115
Burke, Carolyn 57, 117
business enterprises 100
business studies 58